Samurai

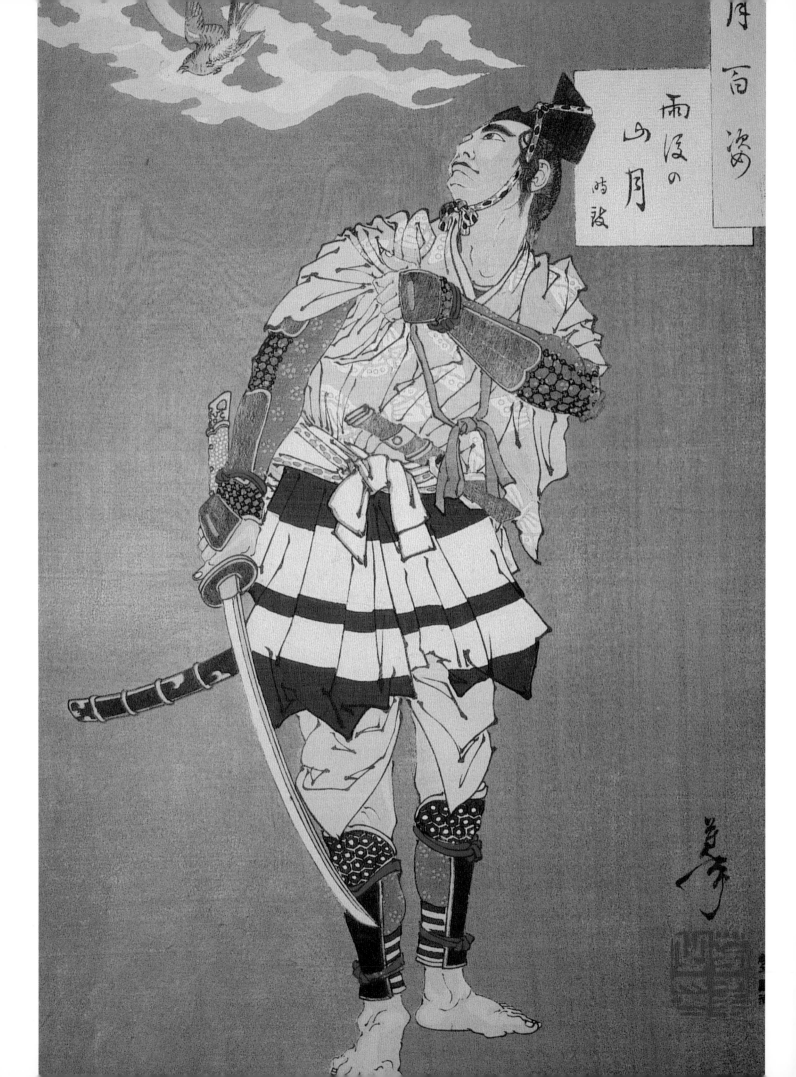

Samurai

The Story of Japan's Great Warriors

Stephen Turnbull

METRO BOOKS
New York

METRO BOOKS
New York

An Imprint of Sterling Publishing
387 Park Avenue South
New York, NY 10016

Dedication: To Richard Robinson, with best wishes and thanks.

Picture Credits: The publisher wishes to thank Stephen Turnbull for kindly supplying all the photography in this book from his picture library Japan Archive: www.stephenturnbull.com

ISBN 978-1-4351-5159-8

For information about custom editions, special sales, and premium and corporate purchases, please contact Sterling Special Sales at 800-805-5489 or specialsales@sterlingpublishing.com.

Manufactured in China

2 4 6 8 10 9 7 5 3 1

www.sterlingpublishing.com

CONTENTS

PREFACE AND ACKNOWLEDGMENTS

The samurai developed as a professional military caste who were at once a military aristocracy and a political ruling class.

This book tells the story of one of the world's greatest military traditions: the samurai of Japan. Having their origins in the warriors of ancient Japan, the samurai developed as a professional military caste who were at once a military aristocracy and a political ruling class. Yet they never left their martial traditions behind, even when the civil wars finished in 1615 and there were no more battles to fight.

For two more centuries the samurai spirit lived on through the martial arts and enjoyed a final flourish with the bitter, yet little known, wars of the Meiji Restoration that created modern Japan.

I wish to thank all who have helped me with this book, in particular the museums, castles, universities, and institutions in Japan that assisted me during my study tour in 2003.

Right: The growing of rice is a vital part of Japanese culture. Here we see the young rice seedlings being transplanted by hand—a method that would have been seen during the time of the samurai.

INTRODUCTION

the world before the samurai

There were people living in Japan long before the word "samurai" was used for a Japanese warrior.

Right: A timeless scene in a Japanese shrine, as a festival performer dressed as a samurai walks by carrying a large umbrella.

Japan in Outline

Japan consists of four main islands and numerous other smaller ones. The largest island is called Honshu, which stretches from north to south. Shikoku island is divided from Honshu by the picturesque Inland Sea. The large southern island of Kyushu is separated from the southern tip of Honshu by the narrow straits of Shimonoseki. The northern island of Hokkaido was not settled until late in samurai history, so it will hardly figure at all in our story. The islands of Japan are located to the east of the Asiatic land mass.

Although apparently isolated, cultural contact with China and Korea has been maintained for centuries through both peaceful and warlike means. The shortest passage to mainland Asia is via Korea. From the Japanese island of Kyushu the two islands of Iki and Tsushima have provided useful staging points for travel between Japan and Korea.

On two occasions in Japanese history the locations of Tsushima and Iki were exploited for military reasons. The first saw the two attempts by Khublai Khan's Mongol armies to invade Japan. In 1274, a raid provided a reconnaissance in force. In 1281, a serious attempt at invasion was thwarted by the *kamikaze*, the "divine wind" that destroyed the invaders' fleet. Three centuries later in 1592, a Japanese invasion force used Iki and Tsushima to cross the straits and invade Korea.

The first permanent capital of Japan was Nara. From here the court moved to Kyoto in A.D. 894, and Kyoto stayed as the capital until it was supplanted by modern Tokyo. Tokyo was formerly known as Edo and was the capital of the Tokugawa shoguns. From the early seventeenth century onward, Edo became the model for the castle town, the entity through which Japan was ruled.

Early Japan and the Jomon, Yayoi, and Kofun Cultures

There were people living in Japan long before the word "samurai" was used for a Japanese warrior. Evidence of human inhabitation of Japan has been identified as far back as 100,000 B.C., but it is not certain whether or not these people were the ancestors of the modern Japanese. But, as time went by, two distinctive pottery producing cultures emerged. The first were the Jomon people, who were primarily hunters and gatherers. Their name means "rope pattern" from their pottery style that involved making rope impressions in the wet clay. Their pots, which carbon dating has shown to be the world's oldest known pottery, were built up from coils of clay and fired at a low temperature. The rope decoration could often produce impressive artistic effects.

Jomon culture bears some relationship to the culture of the aboriginal Japanese Ainu people, some of whom still survive in Hokkaido. The Ainu are probably the descendants of tribesmen who once occupied large parts of the Japanese islands and were driven north in the process described in this chapter. Their physical appearance is different from the average Japanese, as they have lighter skin, more body

Evidence of human inhabitation of Japan has been identified as far back as 100,000 B.C.

Left: Early Japanese pit dwellings from the archaeological site of Yoshinogari in Kyushu. They are reconstructed based on finds from the Yayoi period (300 B.C.–A.D. 300).

hair, a heavier brow ridge and eyes which are sometimes blue or gray. They are probably related to Siberian groups such as the Gilyak.

Unlike the Jomon peoples, however, the other overlapping pottery culture called the Yayoi (c. 300 B.C.–A.D. 300) was associated with people who are clearly identified with the modern Japanese. They cultivated rice and produced pots that were plainer but more technically advanced than those of the Jomon people. The pots were fired at a higher temperature. They also used tools made of metal that were probably imported from mainland China and Korea. These included iron shovels and ploughs, but bronze mirrors and bell-like ritual objects were also an important part of their lives.

A Chinese chronicle describes a Japanese queen called Pimiko who ruled a kingdom in northern Kyushu, possibly like the one discovered at Yoshinogari. The same chronicle mentions in particular Queen Pimiko's burial rites, whereby "a great mound was raised over her more than a hundred paces in diameter and over a hundred of her male and female attendants followed her in death." Such mounds gave a name to the next named historical period, the Kofun (A.D. 200–700). Many of these huge earthen tombs in which local kings and chieftains were buried still exist, and are awe-inspiring from their sheer size and layout. They were often keyhole shaped and occupied a huge area of land. Armor, harness, weapons, bronze mirrors, and jewels were buried along with the deceased. On top or inside the tombs were placed *haniwa*, primitive but lifelike clay models of soldiers, servants, and animals, which may have their origins as substitutes for the human sacrifice described in the account of Queen Pimiko's death. The study of *haniwa* has given us a good picture of life in the Kofun period. Together with the real weapons that were buried in the tombs, the *haniwa* show that these early aristocrats eventually became mounted warriors—ancestors of the samurai.

The articles found inside the tombs indicate both a sophisticated production system in Japan and close trading links with continental Asia. From the fourth century, in fact, Japan seems to have had a colony in Korea called Mimana. It was administered by the current rulers of Japan who were steadily increasing their hegemony throughout Japan. They called themselves the Yamato. By the fourth century most of the former independent kingdoms had become vassals of the Yamato. The Yamato rulers are enormously important in Japanese history as they were the progenitors of the imperial house. Essentially they were simply the most successful warrior chiefs. However, a more colorful account of how the emperor system arose is preserved in mythology.

The Establishment of the Emperor System

Early Japanese history is so shrouded in mystery that to understand the nation's origins we have to consider the great creation myths, along with the revelations uncovered by archaeology. Sometime around the eighth century, the rulers of the Yamato state ordered these myths to be written down as a way of confirming their legitimacy.

Right: The Sanjusangendo in Kyoto, one of the most historic buildings in Japan's ancient capital. This building has survived from the twelfth century. The external eaves shown here are the site of an ancient archery contest.

The most important of these legends tells of the creation of the islands of Japan by the *kami* (gods) Izanagi and Izanami. From them were born the three greatest *kami*: Amaterasu, the Sun Goddess and ruler of heaven; Susano-o, the *kami* of the oceans; and Tsukuyomi, the goddess of darkness and the moon. But there was dissent between Amaterasu and Susano-o, and one day Susano-o went on a drunken rampage. He frightened his sister so much that she hid in a cave and refused to come out. This meant that the world was deprived of light, so various ploys were tried to entice her back. Eventually a female *kami* performed a ribald dance that caused great laughter. Amaterasu was intrigued as to what was going on, and was told that a *kami* superior to her had appeared. Amaterasu peeped out of the cave to see a reflection of

herself in a mirror, and as she emerged further out she was seized. Light was therefore restored to the world, and the mirror that had played such an important role was destined to become part of the Japanese imperial regalia.

The second item in the three Japanese crown jewels enters the story with subsequent events. Susano-o was banished for his bad behavior, and while he was wandering in the land of Izumo he was told that an eight-headed dragon was terrorizing the neighborhood. Susano-o disposed of the dragon by getting it drunk on *sake* (rice wine) and cutting off its eight heads. In its tail he found a sword, which he then presented to his sister as a peace offering. This sword was to become the second item of imperial regalia. The third item was added to the crown jewels when Amaterasu made the

Left: The rice harvest. This autumnal scene sums up the goal of much of the conflict seen in the days of the samurai. The need was to control the rice fields to create wealth.

the Yamato from heaven. Other traditions indicate a more mundane origin, such as a conquest of Japan by horse-riding nomads from Korea, Japan's nearest neighbor, during the latter half of the fourth century A.D. The horse riders' leaders then became the Yamato monarchs.

This has never been a popular theory in Japan. It is significant that one of Japan's most cherished myths is that an invasion did occur about this time, but in the opposite direction, when the Japanese Empress Jingu invaded Korea. She was pregnant when she fought, and later gave birth to the future Emperor Ojin, who was to be deified as Hachiman, the god of war. Hachiman became an enormously powerful deity to the samurai, and many clans adopted him as their tutelary spirit. The invasion in which he was supposed to have taken part as an unborn child was also to be invoked in the future to justify further Japanese aggression overseas. Whatever the truth about the horse-rider theory, it is beyond any doubt that the relations between Japan and Korea at this time were of crucial importance in shaping Japan's history, and also in determining the future direction in which the samurai would develop.

Shinto, Buddhism, and the Asuka Period

Religion, up until this time, was exclusively concerned with the creation myths that provided the basis for the religious system now known as Shinto. Shinto, "the way of the gods," may be regarded as Japan's indigenous religion. It involves the worship of thousands of *kami*

momentous decision to send her grandson Ninigi no mikoto down to earth to rule the world. Along with the mirror and the sword Ninigi was given a curved jewel, which he in turn passed on to his grandson, the first Japanese Emperor Jimmu.

Notwithstanding their historical shortcomings, these stories undoubtedly have some real value in the picture they paint of how the first rulers of Japan, the Yamato monarchs, spread their influence throughout the islands by military means. Certain images to be associated with the samurai, particularly that of the sword, make their initial appearance in the stories. Where these first rulers actually came from is a great area of controversy. The Japanese creation myths suggest a descent of

Left: The Inner Shrine of the Great Shrine of Ise, the holiest place in Shinto, Japan's indigenous religion. Shinto means "the way of the gods."

(deities), who are enshrined at the instantly recognizable Shinto shrines that are dotted all over Japan. The *kami* govern natural forces, and many are intimately linked with agriculture and fertility. Others are associated with special natural features of a landscape, or are spirits of the notable dead, such as the courtier Sugawara Michizane, who was deified as Tenjin, the *kami* of learning. The polytheistic nature of traditional Shinto is important. Though the imperial creation myths allowed the Yamato line to insist that the descendants of the Sun Goddess should be regarded as the most important national *kami*, Shinto still has a marked local flavor. Even today it is the local *kami* who are celebrated in a community's most serious rituals.

But while Kofun tombs were still being built by local rulers in eastern Japan, a rival to the centrality of Shinto was on its way when Buddhism was introduced from Korea. By the time Buddhism reached Japan in A.D. 538 it was already one thousand years old. It appeared in Japan in the form of a small image of the Buddha. It was a gift from the Korean king to the Japanese court, and although it would be many years before Buddhist doctrines would be fully understood in the Japanese context, certain courtiers immediately saw the political potential of the new religion.

Instead of the previously fragmentary and totally decentralized worship of numerous local *kami*, Buddhism promised a unifying force that could provide a path toward creating a new religious framework. This would consist of a single hierarchical system under one central omnipotent deity.

The powerful and ambitious leaders of the Soga clan were the greatest enthusiasts for this viewpoint. They pressed for the adoption of Buddhism, but did not shrink from using violence to further their goals. So Buddhism became a matter of great controversy, as did the

Korean king's gift, which ended up being unceremoniously dumped into a canal. It was soon retrieved, and is now housed within the great Zenkoji temple in Nagano.

The war for Buddhism ended in a victory in A.D. 587 for Umako, the head of the Soga clan. He died in A.D. 626, having ruled through his niece the Empress Suiko. But in spite of Soga Umako's decisive role in establishing Buddhism in Japan, another name is far more closely associated with the spread of Buddhism. This was Prince Shotoku (A.D. 572–621), who ruled as regent from A.D. 593. Shotoku declared Buddhism to be the state religion in Japan. Of all the many Buddhist foundations associated with

Shotoku's religious and political reforms, none is more celebrated than the beautiful temple of Horyuji near Nara, the world's oldest wooden building.

But Prince Shotoku was unable to create a dynasty with such ease. He named his son crown prince, but this was opposed by the new head of the Soga clan, and the unfortunate youth was forced to commit suicide. Revenge was taken by a certain Nakatomi Kamatari (A.D. 614–669), whose clan had been ousted from power a generation earlier by the Soga. His plots came to fruition with the murder of the head of the Soga clan in A.D. 645. The imperial line was now secure, and "kingmaker" Kamatari changed his family name to Fujiwara, after the "grove of wisteria" where he and the crown prince had done their plotting. The name of Fujiwara was to become one of the greatest names in Japanese history.

In A.D. 646, the government announced the Taika reforms, an ambitious set of edicts that theoretically made all of Japan subject to the emperor. One of the first tasks of the reform was to establish Japan's first permanent capital city. This was achieved after a couple of false starts at Nara in A.D. 710. During the Nara period Buddhist art began to flourish in Japan, including the building of structures such as the Todaiji and its Great Buddha, which still bear testimony to the glory of Nara to this day.

Opposite page, top: The Shinto shrine at Kumano, another of the major religious sites of Japan. Kumano represents the end point for a traditional religious pilgrimage that was carried out over hundreds of years by people ranging from emperors to common townsfolk.

Opposite page, bottom: Buddhist priests. The introduction of Buddhism was a very significant moment in Japanese culture. Buddhism did not replace Shinto. Instead both sets of religious beliefs existed harmoniously side by side for most of samurai history.

Left: A Japanese businessman prays for success at the tomb of the Forty-Seven Loyal Retainers at the Sengakuji, Tokyo.

CHAPTER 1

the samurai in early japanese history

Although the actual use of the word samurai does not appear in written records until the twelfth century A.D., it must not be thought Japan had no military tradition before that date.

Right: The samurai Yamanaka Yukimori, celebrated for his loyal support of the doomed Amako family, is commemorated by this statue of him at Toda Castle.

Opposite page: The *ninja*, the undercover warriors of old Japan, recreated here at the castle of Iga Ueno. He is holding a sickle and chain weapon.

Below: A *haniwa* (clay figurine) dressed in the *lamellar keiko* style of armor.

The Ancestors of the Samurai

The word "samurai" usually conjures up an image of an elite mounted archer, skilled in the ways of sword and bow. But although the actual use of the word to describe a Japanese warrior does not appear in written records until the twelfth century A.D., it must not be thought that Japan had no military tradition before that date. By that time the country had already experienced a millennium of warfare fought by men who may be easily identified as the ancestors of the samurai. In fact, so close are the parallels between the early mounted archers and those who were later called samurai, that there is an overpowering argument for regarding the whole evolution of Japan's military as one long continuous development. Rather than simply appearing in the twelfth century, the evidence strongly suggests that in Japan the samurai had always been around in some form.

The Rise of the Mounted Warrior

As the *haniwa* found in the Kofun period tombs suggested, the aristocracy buried in the mounds eventually acted as mounted warriors. However, this was a process that took some time. Just as mainland Asia was involved in friendly cultural contacts with Japan, so it played a part in the development of warfare.

The situation in Korea gave Japan some of its first experiences of warfare. For the first six centuries of the Christian era, the Korean peninsula was divided between the three rival kingdoms of Koguryo, Paekche, and Silla. The largest state was Koguryo whose territory covered nearly all of what is now North Korea. At its height Koguryo stretched well into Manchuria and took in the Liaodong peninsula. The Paekche kingdom was based around the fertile Han River near present day Seoul, and controlled most of the western half of South Korea. Silla emerged during the fifth century, and ruled the eastern provinces. Over the years each of the three kingdoms alternately formed alliances with each other and fought for dominance. Kinship ties and the physical closeness of Japan to Korea meant that this was a conflict in which Japan was heavily involved. The Japanese fielded expeditionary armies who initially only fought on foot using bows, swords, and spears.

In about A.D. 400 a Japanese army, sent to support Paekche and composed entirely of foot soldiers, was heavily defeated in battle in Korea by a Koguryo army riding on horses. Although horses were already being used in Japan as beasts of burden, this battle was Japan's first encounter with cavalry, and the experience was to be a profound one. Some historians link this event to the eventual conquest of Japan by these same horse riders whom legend was to transform into the heavenly founders of the Japanese monarchy. Whatever the truth, within a century of this event there is archaeological evidence of horses being ridden in Japan. The first component of the samurai tradition was now established.

The plains of eastern Japan proved ideal ground for horse breeding and pasturing and, as riding skills developed, so did the notion of

cavalry warfare, with mounted archery coming to be the preferred technique. In A.D. 553, Paekche once again sought Japanese help. They asked particularly for "a large supply of bows and horses," thus indicating that the combination of horsemanship and archery was now firmly in place.

In A.D. 602, a Japanese prince called Prince Kume led an expedition to Korea at the head of a force which was almost a prototype of the later samurai armies. Its officers were local chieftains who bore titles such as *kuni no miyatsuko* (local servants of the Court). There were between 120 and 150 of these chieftains in existence. The Yamato rulers had chosen them as their regional arm, and the Court supported their local autonomy in return for tribute. These men had the wealth and resources to become elite mounted archers, and were followed into battle by a much larger number of foot soldiers.

The social position and role of these powerful local landowners suggests close

Above: Kusunoki Masashige was a mounted warrior in the fourteenth century. Here he is depicted on a fine equestrian statue near the site of his birth.

parallels with the later samurai. This identification is strengthened by accounts of a rebellion led by one of these men, Tsukushi no Kimi Iwai, in A.D. 572. Iwai is believed to have been bribed by the Silla kingdom not to lead a Japanese army to Korea to do battle for the Paekche. His defiance soon turned into an open rebellion against the Yamato monarch, who was forced to send another regional strong man against him, and Iwai was defeated.

Right: Minamoto Yoshiie dressed in the long flowing robes of an archer of the Nara court, where inspiration came from China.

Challenges from China

Further wars continued to occur in Korea, and before long China also became directly involved. For the past 350 years, China had existed as a number of small states which were finally united in A.D. 589 under the Sui dynasty. Koguryo was its immediate neighbor and having cultivated good relations with Paekche and Silla, the Sui emperor decided to invade Koguryo in A.D. 612. The attempt was a disaster. The defeat was devastating in the Chinese political field as well, as internal rebellions broke out and the short-lived Sui dynasty was eclipsed by the Tang in A.D. 618. It took a few years before the Tang felt secure enough to turn their attention against Koguryo, and in A.D. 645 they followed Sui's example with an invasion led by the Emperor Tang Taizong.

This was also a failure, but the developments on the continent were alarming to Japan. So seriously were they regarded that in that same year there was a military coup in Japan. A new Japanese emperor arose who was determined to set his country on a sound military footing. An army based on a centralized model like Tang China was seen as being the ideal. Emperor Kotoku began collecting weapons and putting them under state control. This was not the last time in Japanese history that such a move was contemplated. The only people who were permitted to keep their arms were those who faced attacks from the *emishi* in northeastern Japan.

Meanwhile the Korean situation grew more serious. Tang China realized that to destroy Koguryo they had to first neutralize any support that Koguryo might receive from Paekche. The other kingdom, Silla, threw in its lot with the Tang. They made an agreement in A.D. 660 for a Tang naval landing to support a Silla attack on Paekche, who were still supported by Japan. General Kim Yu-shin (A.D. 595–673), who defeated the Paekche army at the battle of Puyo, led the Silla army. But when the King of Paekche surrendered, his followers continued to fight and asked for help from their Japanese allies, who sent three expeditionary armies

Left: Mounted archers of the Nara period, dressed in full court robes. These men were the first samurai.

across the sea to Korea in A.D. 661, 662, and 663. At first the war to aid Paekche went well, but, uniting their forces, the Tang and Silla armies moved against their enemies at the battle of the Paekch'on River. In this encounter, partly fought from rival warships, the Japanese suffered the worst defeat of their early history. As many as 10,000 men were killed, and many ships and horses were lost.

The defeat at the Paekch'on River caused much heart searching among the Japanese. Had they relied too much on individual skill and bravery? Had the Chinese overwhelmed them by using well-organized infantry tactics, a

mode of warfare to which Emperor Kotoku had been inclined? Was mounted warfare perhaps inappropriate after all? Japan was now firmly embroiled in East Asian politics, and her warrior traditions and techniques needed to be seriously questioned.

It was not long before the fear of an invasion of Japan from Korea reached its height. In A.D. 666 the Tang invaded northern Korea and laid siege to the Koguryo capital of P'yongyang. The city fell after a month-long siege and 20,000 prisoners were taken. The Tang were eager to make the whole of Korea their vassal state, so a war between Tang and

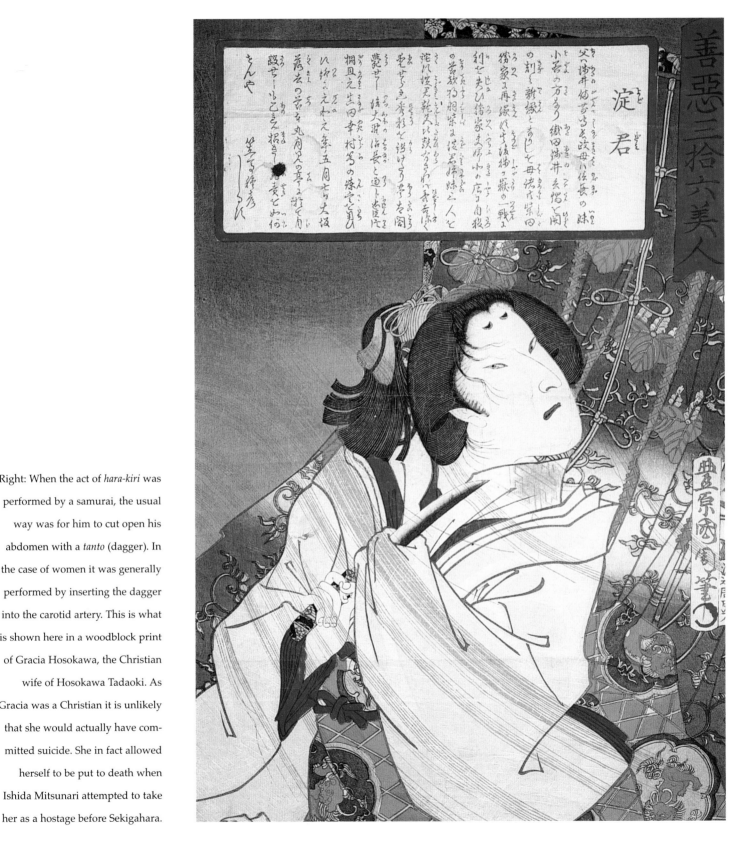

Right: When the act of *hara-kiri* was performed by a samurai, the usual way was for him to cut open his abdomen with a *tanto* (dagger). In the case of women it was generally performed by inserting the dagger into the carotid artery. This is what is shown here in a woodblock print of Gracia Hosokawa, the Christian wife of Hosokawa Tadaoki. As Gracia was a Christian it is unlikely that she would actually have committed suicide. She in fact allowed herself to be put to death when Ishida Mitsunari attempted to take her as a hostage before Sekigahara.

their old ally Silla began. When neither side gained the upper hand, negotiations were held which allowed Silla to control almost the whole of the Korean peninsula. Japan was now threatened by a hostile alliance of Silla and China, so the ruling emperor Tenji took steps to confront the challenge. In A.D. 670, Emperor Tenji ordered a nationwide census of Japan as a first step toward introducing a conscript army on the Chinese model. He began fortifying the northern Kyushu coast, the area where an invasion would be likely to land. Guards and beacons were also posted on the two islands of Tsushima and Iki in the Korean Strait.

When war finally came, it came not through invasion but within Japan itself. When Emperor Tenji died in A.D. 671, his succession was disputed and a civil war broke out between his two sons in A.D. 672. The victor ascended the throne as Emperor Temmu. Although both sides used infantry armies in their battles, much of Temmu's triumph lay in his employment of mounted units to seize strategic locations. Many of these mounted contingents were supplied by powerful local landowners, as had happened in the past.

With his throne secure, Emperor Temmu faced up to the twin challenges of foreign invasion and the power of these local chieftains—some of whom had supported him and some of whom had followed his brother. The result was one of the most far-reaching attempts to reform the military system in the whole of Japanese history. Appreciating that he would always be both dependent upon the regional forces and threatened by them, Temmu issued a decree in

A.D. 684 ordering all civil and military officials in his Court to become skilled in the martial arts, because "in government, military matters are the essential thing." These men would be the core of his army against invasion, and could control any recalcitrant regional official who was not acting loyally.

To ensure this overwhelming central control, Temmu, like his predecessor Kotoku in A.D. 645, began the confiscation of weapons from anyone not employed in his government. These would be issued to the conscript infantrymen. Korea was still a threat, and because during his own rebellion Temmu had made good use of the warriors from eastern Japan, the land of horses, he began recruiting these fine soldiers as border guards in preparation for the coming invasion. Many mounted archers were therefore to find themselves many miles from home as they were moved from one end of Japan to the other, and poems exist that tell of their sadness on leaving loved ones for service hundreds of miles away.

The Conscript Armies

Temmu's successors continued his work. The military reforms culminated in A.D. 702 with the Taiho system, which finally succeeded in creating a large and reliable Japanese army conscripted on the Chinese model. The idea was that the army would be a largely infantry based force, armed with the latest weapon technology, including crossbows. These troops would then be drafted to the area around the imperial capital of Nara or to the fortresses of Kyushu. A

Temmu had made good use of the warriors from eastern Japan, the land of horses.

heishi (soldier) was assigned to a particular gundan (regiment), and served for part of the year, the rest of the time was spent on agricultural duties. Every soldier carried a bow and quiver and had a pair of swords. Much use was made of heavy wooden shields as battlefield protection.

It was a model that had much to recommend it, being relatively inexpensive and as independent as possible of the local chieftains, but circumstances were against it being fully implemented. The defense of Japan was not being written on a blank sheet of paper. The local powerful landowners still existed, and controlled the crucial horse pasture lands. Even though an attempt was made in A.D. 721 to limit the number of horses owned by men outside the Court, the ultimate framework of the army was something of a compromise between the new Chinese model and the well-established Japanese practice of elite mounted archers leading poorly disciplined peasants. This old system had suited the interests of those who controlled it and these archers were undoubtedly good soldiers. This is shown by the fact that Temmu himself had used them for his own purposes and then made them the key component of his coastal defense system.

The weakness in the system was the government's inability to guarantee the loyalty of the local powerful landowners. This was

Left: A samurai general sits surrounded by his followers. Note the *ashigaru* whose job it is to carry equipment in the lacquered boxes.

dramatically illustrated in A.D. 740 when Fujiwara Hirotsugu revolted. He was eventually overcome by a Court army, but it is interesting to note that both sides used armies that were commanded by leaders drawn from a similar stock of local powerful landowners, rather than the government's own conscript infantry.

In A.D. 756, a further example of military power employed in Court politics was shown in the events following the death of Emperor Shomu. Fujiwara Nakamaro took the part of one of the succession candidates and engaged in open warfare. Fujiwara was by no means the legalistic, learned Chinese-style bureaucrat that is commonly associated with the Nara Court, but was a skilled military leader, who used his personal ties and connections to encourage

loyalty to him, as well as to the imperial court. The result was that Fujiwara Nakamaro commanded what was effectively his own private army. The age of the samurai was not far off.

The Eastern Barbarians

As the threat of Korean invasion receded under the Unified Silla state, the attentions of the Nara Court were once again drawn to a matter which had caused their predecessors much concern at various times in history. In the northeast of Japan lived people referred to as the *emishi*, a word that usually had the connotation of "barbarian," but their exact origins is still obscure. Expeditions to subdue the barbarians appear in the earliest myths about Japan's Yamato

Opposite page, top: The race across the Uji River during the second battle of Uji in 1184. To be the first into battle was one of the great samurai ideals, and on this occasion two rivals were not going to let a little thing like a river stand in their way! This was an old samurai tradition.

Opposite page, bottom: The *tsuki mabisashi* style of helmet associated with the *keiko* style of armor. The heavy peak is typical. The circular disc on top was probably intended to carry a plume.

In A.D. 709, the temporarily pacified barbarians revolted against control from distant Nara, and a further insurrection in A.D. 724 took eight months to quell.

In A.D. 737, a large expedition under Ono no Azumibito succeeded somewhat in pacifying the area, and the government's policy of settlement continued. But in A.D. 774, another major revolt began. The conscripts of the Chinese-style army marched north in their thousands accompanied by the elite mounted archers of the Court, but the *emishi* adopted guerrilla tactics and harassed the Nara troops from the mountains and valleys with which they were so familiar. Unlike the straight swords of the Nara soldiers, the *emishi* used curved blades which were more effective from the saddle, a model that was later to become the badge of the samurai class. Lightly armored and highly mobile, the mounted archers of the *emishi* took on their rivals as the conscripts moved in sluggish formations in their heavy armor. Arrows were sent into their ranks, and the *emishi* then disappeared into the forests. The battle of Koromogawa in A.D. 789 proved to be almost as much of a disaster as the battle of the Paekch'on River had been, where many of the Nara conscripts were drowned in the river.

It took 40 years for the strength in numbers possessed by the Court to allow them to overcome the *emishi.* In A.D. 796, the Nara Court's leader who had borne the brunt of the fighting, Sakanoue no Tamuramaro, was given the title of "Great Barbarian-Subduing General" or *sei i tai shogun*, an expression that was later to be used for the overall leader of the samurai. He

Above: A courtier of the Nara period, where bureaucracy ruled the military.

monarchs, who coveted their land, using "civilization" as a well-worn excuse to make war upon them. The first authentic records of fighting against the *emishi* occurs in A.D. 658, when the fear of Korea was also at its height.

Left: The strategic islands of Iki and Tsushima helped defend Japan during the ninth century. This bas-relief depicts the horrors of the Mongol invasion in Fukuoka, during the attack on the island of Iki in 1274.

was but one of the many leaders to receive rewards of land for their role. Most of them also had their social origins in the same local chieftains whom successive governments had sought to control, but who in the end proved indispensable. When hostilities with the *emishi* ceased and the Nara government began to take a good look at their armies, the decision had virtually been made for them. The peasant conscript armies had been a failure, and once again the greatest service had been rendered by the local warriors whose skills and experience had been further honed by the barbarian conflicts. This was to be the exclusive direction that successive emperors would look when recruiting in future. The system of conscripting peasants finally ended in A.D. 792. The official

reason was that a decision had been made to reduce the burden on farming communities of impressed labor. There was much truth in this, and it had long been recognized that if the household breadwinner was drafted then the whole family would suffer. There was even a saying that if a man was conscripted for *heishi* duties then he was unlikely to return until his hair had turned white! But with the pacification of the *emishi,* and improved relations with Korea under the Unified Silla state, Japan's borders were now more secure than they had been for centuries. In A.D. 835, even the guards that were mounted on the strategic islands of Iki and Tsushima were withdrawn, and the famous sad poems, written home by soldiers, now became a thing of the past.

Yet with the passing of external threats the Court realized that it could not let itself be undefended. There had been enough rebellions in the past to cause real concern for the future, and if there was to be no conscription, who would provide security for Nara and its successor Heian (Kyoto) which became the capital in A.D. 894? The answer was found in the recruitment of *kondei* (strong fellows), warriors who were not commoners but were the descendants of the same class of local powerful landowners who had been Japan's military elite for hundreds of years. The edict of A.D. 792 specified that each *kondei* should be supported by two grooms who would also act as foot soldiers, the same individual structure that was later to be associated with the samurai.

Rewards and Rebels

The recruitment of elite warriors meant that by around A.D. 860 most of the characteristics of the Japanese samurai were already in place. There existed a military arm on whom the government relied who rode horses, used bows, wielded curved swords, and passed their wealth and military traditions on to their sons. All that was missing was political power.

At first all was well, and when rebels arose or succession disputes happened, the *kondei* were content to do their duty for the imperial court and receive their just rewards, but it was not long before a different challenge to the system was made. In A.D. 866, a minor incident occurred at the Hirono River, when rival district magistrates from the Mino and Owari provinces fought a battle over a border dispute. The significance of the incident is that neither side had any hesitation about using the official government military forces at their disposal for settling a local domestic quarrel.

The district magistrates involved in the Hironogawa battle were of course from the same social grouping of *kondei*, the "powerful

The recruitment of elite warriors meant that by around A.D. 860 most of the characteristics of the Japanese samurai were already in place.

Right: Samurai swear loyalty to their lord in this ink painted scroll from the Hyogo Prefectural Museum.

local landowner" or "local chieftain" stock, and the appointment to such offices as district magistrate was fiercely competitive. The ninth century was also a time of economic decline that was marked by plagues and episodes of starvation—all factors that led to resentment against the central government which a landowner could exploit to his advantage. Tax collection, family ties to the Court, rewards for service, and rivalry over official appointments all merged in a system that favored the strong and the rich, and saw them grow stronger and richer. Riots, lawlessness, and localized opportunistic rebellions began to plague Japan, and, by the beginning of the tenth century, the government was forced to grant far-reaching powers to its provincial governors to levy troops and act on their own initiatives when disorder threatened. This was the time when we first see the use of the term "samurai," which literally means "those who serve," being used in a purely military context. At first it referred to men who went up to the capital to provide guard duty.

Left: One of the most famous and celebrated samurai in all Japanese history was the loyal Kusunoki Masashige, who committed suicide after his defeat at the battle of Minatogawa in 1336. Here we see him with his war horse. His flag has his embroidered *mon* (badge) of a chrysanthemum on the water. He sits on a tiger-skin rug.

Right: This woodblock print shows the samurai general Minamoto Yoshitsune in action during the battle of Yashima in 1184 when he defeated the Taira. He is depicted jumping on to an enemy ship. His helmet is set off by long golden *kuwagata* (antlers). His *tachi* (sword) is slung from his belt inside a tiger-skin-covered scabbard, but Yoshitsune's weapon of choice is a *naginata* (glaive).

The first major test for the system happened in A.D. 935 with the revolt of Taira Masakado. He was the descendant of Prince Takamochi, an imperial prince who had been sent to the Kanto to quell disorders and had been granted the surname of "Taira," which may be translated as "the pacifier." The Taira clan grew to be so important that a succession dispute within this one family could provoke the serious armed conflict that was carried out between Masakado and his rivals. At first the Heian Court regarded it as a minor local affair, but as the fighting grew so did the wide range of issues for which Masakado claimed to be striving, aims which reached the dizzy heights of Masakado proclaiming himself as the "new emperor." An army supplied at a provincial level eventually overcame the Masakado rebellion, and Masakado was beheaded in A.D. 940. A similarly serious insurrection led by Fujiwara Sumitomo on the Inland Sea to the west of Kyoto also ended with him being beheaded.

Two particular points of interest arise out of these rebellions. First, they were conducted by warriors who led elite mounted horsemen and also many foot soldiers, the compromise pattern of military organization that had been emerging over the past few centuries. Second, their social origins were becoming increasingly well defined as a local aristocracy that had links both to the Heian Court and to well-established warrior houses in the provinces. In addition to the names of Taira and Fujiwara, which appear on both sides of both rebellions, we may also note the appearance of the Minamoto family on to the Japanese scene.

The social networks that existed between the centralized Heian government and the provinces were of utmost importance, whether their members were maintaining guard duty and performing a policing role in the capital or keeping the peace away from it. A complex linkage of loyalty, blood ties, and rewards supported a system that seemed to operate in the interests of all law-abiding inhabitants of Japan, and may with some justification be regarded as a success. Yet even high-born aristocrats could be troublesome on occasions. All of the high ranking samurai on duty in the capital had brought with them servants and attendants who owed loyalty to their masters, so disputes between rival warriors occurred. These incidents were as often as not resolved by violence, with arrows flying in the Kyoto streets.

So exclusive did these warrior houses become that anyone who presumed to wield a bow in the service of the emperor and could not demonstrate that he was of the lineage of a military house stood little chance of promotion or advancement. In 1028, for example, Fujiwara Norimoto was condemned for being

Below: Minamoto Kiso Yoshinaka, depicted here in a statue at the site of his victory of Kurikara in 1183.

"not of warrior blood" in spite of his impressive surname and recognized martial accomplishments. By contrast, in 1046 Minamoto Yorinobu could reel off a pedigree that went back twenty-one generations to Emperor Ojin. Such a lineage was every bit as important as Yorinobu's undoubted military skills "in the way of horse and bow." He had demonstrated these very effectively in his role as governor of Hitachi province when he quelled the rebellion of Taira Tadatsune around 1016. This is an important date, because it was the first time that the two famous houses of Taira and Minamoto met in battle.

Minamoto Yorinobu's local power base was a complex one knitted together by aristocratic descent, ties of marriage, and long service. These factors were frequently enhanced because of opportunism from other local landowners who wished to associate themselves with a strong and successful military leader with an admirable pedigree. Success bred success, and within 20 years Minamoto Yorinobu's son Yoriyoshi was to become engaged in a conflict that set his family on the road toward greatness. This was the *Zenkunen no eki* (The Former Nine Years' War), which lasted from 1051 to 1062.

This curiously named conflict was the first major war to be fought in the northeast of Japan since the great upheavals associated with the *emishi* described earlier. On one side was Abe Yoritoki, whose family were of *emishi* descent and had held the hereditary post of district magistrate for six generations. His misdemeanor concerned taxes collected by Abe but

not passed on to the central government. Minamoto Yoriyoshi was sent to deal with him, and a peaceful settlement was reached that lasted for a while until an internal dispute within the Abe family descended into violence. Abe Yoritoki then died, and war broke out between his son Abe Sadato and the Minamoto. At first the Abe prevailed, defeating the pro-government forces in 1057, and it was not until 1062 when Minamoto Yoriyoshi persuaded another local strong man called Kiyowara Mitsuyori to join him that Abe was defeated at the battle of Kuriyagawa. Minamoto Yoriyoshi took the rebel's head back to Kyoto in triumph and was richly rewarded.

Riding at Yoriyoshi's side during the Former Nine Years' War was his son Minamoto Yoshiie, who earned great personal glory during the bitter fighting of his father's campaigns and gained for himself the nickname of Hachimantaro, "the first-born son of Hachiman, god of war." The year 1083 was to see this new hero of the Minamoto forging a name for himself in his own right. There was one major difference however, because the so-called *Gosannen no eki* (Later Three Years' War), which was waged by Minamoto Yoshiie against his family's former allies the Kiyowara, was not carried out as a result of an imperial commission to chastise a rebel, but was simply a private feud between the two men.

Much of the fighting of this war took place during the winter in long sieges of the wooden stockades that acted as castles during the eleventh century. Yoshiie found himself in a stalemate situation, largely because the

Success bred success, and within 20 years Minamoto Yorinobu's son Yoriyoshi was to become engaged in a conflict that set his family on the road toward greatness.

government refused to send him any troops for his cause in spite of Yoshiie's claims that Kiyowara was a dangerous rebel. Nor could he levy soldiers locally for what was a private war. So adamant about this were the Heian Court, that when Yoshiie's own brother indicated his intention to leave Kyoto and join Yoshiie he found himself dismissed from office.

In spite of all this the Minamoto were eventually victorious after overcoming the fortress of Kanezawa with much slaughter. Still hoping to convince the government that he had provided a valuable service in quelling a dangerous man, Yoshiie took the heads of the Kiyowara samurai to Kyoto to present them for reward, just as his father had done with the Abe rebels. But the Heian Court stuck to their guns. There could be no reward for the ending of a personal vendetta that the government had never authorized. Angry at being scorned, Yoshiie threw the heads into a nearby ditch. To add insult to injury the Heian Court then brought up the delicate matter that, while the late and supposed rebel Kiyowara had paid all his taxes, the Minamoto still owed them a tidy sum! They also reminded him that ending Abe's tax evasion had been the reason for which his father had once gone to war and had been so richly rewarded. It took Yoshiie ten years to settle the matter, comforted by the thought that even if he was in financial trouble with the Court, at least his martial reputation was secure. Yoshiie was the hero of the samurai.

While the Minamoto were making a name for themselves in the northeast of Japan, their rivals the Taira were acquiring similar glory in the west of the country by quelling the pirates who plagued the Inland Sea. Just as Yoriyoshi had been sent north to suppress Abe's insurrection, so Taira Tadamori received an imperial commission to clear the seas of this other menace to peaceful trade. The expedition was successful, and Tadamori returned with the now customary heads and received his reward.

The Warrior Monks

It was now clear that the Heian Court was becoming highly dependent upon these two powerful lineages of Taira and Minamoto to keep the peace. Members of both families spent much of their time around the capital as well as on these policing duties, and in addition to

Below: Enryakuji, the temple on top of Mount Hiei near Kyoto, that was the headquarters for one of the fiercest armies of warrior monks. On several occasions the monks descended from Mount Hiei to terrify the imperial court.

Right: The vast mountainous interior of central Japan. This was the lair of wandering mountain ascetics, remote villages, and *ninja*.

Below: The view of Mount Hiei looking across from the shore of Lake Biwa. This was an alternative attack route for the warrior monks.

their pirate quelling, the name of Taira became particularly associated with a pacification process of a very different sort. Since the time of the transfer of the capital to Kyoto in A.D. 794 the Court had been subject to the increasing influence of the Buddhist monastic complex located on the summit and flanks of Mount Hiei to the northeast of the city. The Nara Court had greatly valued its Buddhist connections and had richly endowed temples such as the Todaiji and Kofukuji in the old capital of Nara. The Mount Hiei temples, of which the most important was the Enryakuji, added a further dimension through *feng shui* (Chinese geomancy), which maintained that the northeast quarter of a city was the entrance for demons. Mount Hiei was therefore the city's spiritual guardian twice over. The growth in landowning power enjoyed by the warrior families of Taira and Minamoto was matched only by the wealth of these great Buddhist institutions. Great jealousy existed between the temples of Kyoto and Nara over matters of precedence and prestige.

The First Temple Feuds

There was no reason why political disagreements over the affairs of an important religious institution should necessarily lead to armed conflict, but by the middle of the tenth century bitter disputes over imperial control of senior appointments led to brawling between rival monks and eventually to the use of weapons. These inter-temple or inter-faction disputes were not "religious wars" as we know them in

the West. They did not involve points of doctrine or dogma, just politics, and the campaigns and battles of the warrior monks from the tenth to the fourteenth centuries were almost exclusively concerned with rivalries between and within the temples of Nara and Mount Hiei.

Above: A typical little wayside shrine bearing the Buddhist device of a swastika, also used as a family (*mon*) badge by the Hachisuka and Tsugaru families.

Right: The Isonokami Shrine near Tenri. This shrine houses a unique "seven-branched sword" of Korean origin, one of the most important artifacts to survive from the time that Japan enjoyed close relationships with the three kingdoms of Korea.

The first major incident involving violence by monks against monks occurred in A.D. 949, when 56 monks from Nara's Todaiji gathered at the residence of an official in Kyoto to protest against an appointment that had displeased them. At this stage the small band can hardly be called an army of warrior monks, but a brawl ensued during which some participants were killed. In A.D. 968, several demonstrations were targeted against members of the Fujiwara family, but here the weapon was intimidation tinged with religious fear rather than actual violence. The protagonists in this case were the monks of Kofukuji in Nara, the temple that controlled the nearby Kasuga shrine, the clan shrine of the Fujiwara family.

However, in A.D. 969, a dispute over conflicting claims to temple lands resulted in the death of several Kofukuji monks at the hands of

monks from Todaiji. It is almost certain that weapons were carried to this incident and used in the fight—the days of the warrior monk had arrived. It is also around this time, probably during A.D. 970, that Enryakuji is involved in a dispute with the Gion shrine in Kyoto, using force to settle the matter. After this incident Ryogen, the chief abbot of Enryakuji, made the decision to maintain a permanent fighting force at Mount Hiei. This was the first of the warrior monk armies.

Rivalry also existed between the neighboring temples of Enryakuji and Miidera. In 1039 a conflict started when the incumbent abbot of Miidera was appointed to be the new abbot of Enryakuji. Three thousand enraged monks from Mount Hiei poured into Kyoto and descended on the residence of the courtier Fujiwara Yorimichi, who had been largely responsible for

Left: The view of the Uji River (scene of battles in 1180, 1184, and 1221) looking across the river from the Byodo-In temple, where Minamoto Yorimasa committed suicide in 1180.

the decision. When he refused to alter his appointment his gates were kicked in, so the terrified official summoned samurai to restore order and a bloody fight began. The end result was a victory for violence and intimidation, because Yorimichi gave in and named the Mount Hiei candidate as abbot instead. This man died nine years later in 1047, and again Yorimichi tried to enforce a Miidera candidate, but pressure from Enryakuji ensured that the unfortunate man's term of office lasted only three days. In fact, during the twelfth century there were seven attempts to promote abbots from Miidera to Enryakuji, and none succeeded because of intimidation.

Yet in spite of their intense rivalry and frequent conflicts, there were occasions when Enryakuji and Miidera were willing to join forces to attack a third party. Thus, we hear of

them united against Nara's Kofukuji in 1081. During this incident Kofukuji burned Miidera and carried off much loot, but later that same year the alliance seems to have been forgotten when Enryakuji burned Miidera following the shrine festival incident noted above. In 1113 Enryakuji burned the Kiyomizudera in Kyoto over a rival appointment of an abbot.

Disputes then began which set the monks against the Heian Court. The warrior monks soon discovered that a show of force in the capital, carried out by an army of monks wielding their long *naginata* (glaives) and carrying in procession the *mikoshi*, the portable shrines in which the *kami* were believed to dwell, had the effect of frightening the courtiers into granting their wishes for fear of either being beheaded or cursed. The retired emperor Go Shirakawa was quoted as saying that there were only three things that even an emperor could not control: the rapids on the Kamo river, the fall of dice at gambling, and the warrior monks.

It took the warriors from the emerging samurai class to stand up to them. When Minamoto Yorimasa and his men met the monks as they advanced on Kyoto during one of their riots their firm but respectful attitude led the *sohei* to divert their attack elsewhere. In 1146, it was a member of the Taira family who incurred the monastic wrath. This time they found their way to the imperial palace barred by samurai under the command of Taira Kiyomori. With a haughty disregard for religious scruples Kiyomori ordered his men to open fire, and an arrow hit the sacred *mikoshi*.

The monks withdrew, calling down curses upon the house of Taira and vowing to return, but a very valuable point had been made. From this time on the imperial court were full of gratitude toward Taira Kiyomori, who saw his star rise. He had already taken the opportunity of marrying female relatives into the imperial line, and the name of Taira soon became a very prestigious lineage to proclaim on the field of battle.

Taira and Minamoto

So influential did the two families of Taira and Minamoto become that it was not long before their names were to be found involved in a succession dispute that directly concerned the

Right: According to legend, a wandering priest called Mongaku, who was a Minamoto supporter, visited Yoritomo with the skull of Yoritomo's father Yoshitomo to show him the horrible deaths that had been meted out to his family by Taira Kiyomori.

imperial family. This happened in 1156, and the subsequent battle is known as the *Hogen no Ran* (The Hogen Rebellion) from the name of the period during which it took place.

On this occasion the two families did not divide along clan lines. Instead Minamoto Tameyoshi and his son Tametomo, a samurai renowned for the power of his archery, found themselves opposing Tameyoshi's other son Yoshitomo, who was allied with Taira Kiyomori. The fighting of the Hogen Rebellion was very brief and centered around a night attack that was ended with the besieged building being set on fire. Minamoto Tameyoshi was defeated and executed, and his son Tametomo was banished.

In 1160 there was another uprising called the Heiji Rebellion that was carried out on behalf of rival imperial claimants. This time the Taira fought the Minamoto. Yoshitomo, who had seen his own father executed after opposing him during the Hogen Rebellion, led an attack on the Sanjo Palace in Kyoto. Taira Kiyomori, whose absence from the scene had been the cue for the attack, soon hurried back to the capital and defeated Yoshitomo so severely that the Minamoto had to flee for their lives. The Taira pursued them into the mountains. Yoshitomo was tracked down and killed, and to complete his triumph Taira Kiyomori ordered the execution of all the Minamoto supporters who had challenged him. Of the main branch of

Left: The temple of Fudoji, built on the site of Minamoto Yoshinaka's celebrated victory at the battle of Kurikara (Tonamiyama) in 1183 is shown shrouded in mist.

Right: Minamoto Yoritomo, the founder of the Minamoto dynasty of shoguns. The Gempei Wars began in 1180 with an uprising against the Taira by Minamoto Yoritomo, whose life had been spared because he was only a young boy at the time of the Heiji Rebellion in 1161.

shown by the rapid and firm treatment dealt out to a doomed Fujiwara conspiracy in 1177. By 1180, the Taira ruled Japan.

The Gempei Wars

The Gempei Wars, the Great Civil Wars of medieval Japan, were fought from 1180 until 1185, and takes its name from the Chinese readings of the names Minamoto (Gen) and Taira (Hei) who fought against each other. It may be surprising to hear that there were any Minamoto left to oppose the Taira after the executions that followed the Heiji Rebellion, but in 1180 two separate rebellions began in different parts of Japan, each of which was led by a member of a different generation of the Minamoto family. In Kyoto, the leader was the veteran Minamoto Yorimasa, who was now an old man, and who had refused to take sides in the Heiji Rebellion. Far to the east in Izu province the revolt was led by young Minamoto Yoritomo, whose life had been spared by Kiyomori on account of his infancy.

the family only a handful including the veteran warrior Yorimasa and Yoshitomo's young children were spared.

Following his triumph during the Heiji Rebellion, Taira Kiyomori went from strength to strength. In 1167, he attained the title of *Daijo Daijin* (Grand Minister), the highest rank that an emperor could award. Kiyomori was now effectively the ruler of Japan, and seems to have ruled it very well. The seafaring traditions of the Taira led him to encourage trade with Song China, and the family's growing wealth led them to institute a nationwide system of vassalage, thus extending the Taira's military resources far beyond what any warrior family had ever dreamed of. So thorough was their network that potential rebels were summarily dealt with before they had a chance to act, as

The network of vassals who owed loyalty to the Taira should have been sufficient to nip any rising in the bud, and this is exactly what happened in both cases. Yoritomo's movements were followed, and an army of local Taira supporters defeated him at the battle of Ishibashiyama. Yoritomo narrowly escaped with his life and took a boat across what is now Tokyo Bay to the safety of the traditional Minamoto heartlands in the Kanto, the provinces immediately to the east of the Hakone mountains.

Left: Minamoto Yoshitsune at the last battle of the Gempei Wars: the battle of Dan no Ura in 1185, a sea battle when the Taira were decisively defeated.

Minamoto Yorimasa fared no better. He had allied himself with the warrior monks of Miidera, and when the Taira moved against them the Minamoto force made a strategic withdrawal toward Nara, from where they expected a monk army of the Kofukuji to come to their aid. To cover their retreat Minamoto Yorimasa crossed the Uji river and took up a position on its southern bank, having removed a long section of planking from the bridge so that the Taira could not cross and attack them. Early the next morning the Taira horsemen appeared out of the mist on the northern banks of the Uji River, and a fierce archery duel began. A number of individual combats were fought on the parapet of the broken bridge, but the action was stalemated until a number of daring Taira samurai drove their horses into the water and began to swim across. Part of their motivation was a desire for the great honor of being the first into battle, an achievement that was to become a samurai obsession.

Yorimasa and his sons were driven back into the compound of the Byodo-In temple, and when they realized that no Nara monks were coming to help them, and that their rebellion was therefore almost over, Minamoto Yorimasa performed what was to be regarded as the classic act of *hara-kiri.* He was not the first samurai to commit suicide after being defeated, but the way he did it, by first writing a farewell poem on his signaling fan, and then cutting open his abdomen while his sons held off the enemy, set a standard that generations of samurai were to admire for centuries to come.

With two separate Minamoto rebellions safely crushed, the Taira felt very confident about taking the fight to the Minamoto territories in the east. An expedition was put together, and in November 1180 the Taira army encountered the Minamoto somewhere along the Fujigawa, the river that flows down from the area of Mount Fuji to the sea. It was there that an incident took place. It was a tragi-comical event that hardly deserves the title of the battle of Fujigawa—the Taira were encamped beside the river when the sounds of hundreds of water fowl flying over their lines made them think that the Minamoto were launching a night attack. The Taira rapidly withdrew (perhaps not with the panic that is commonly supposed to have occurred) to Kyoto.

Two years of consolidation followed for both sides with some skirmishing. The fighting was even suspended at one stage because of a desperate famine, but by 1183 the Taira felt sufficiently confident to mount another expedition. This time it was to deal with the right flank of the Minamoto threat in the form of Minamoto Yoshinaka, Yoritomo's cousin. He dominated the provinces to the north of Kyoto, and the Taira high command saw an ideal opportunity to deal with him quickly before Yoritomo could come to his aid from the east. The campaign began very well with the fall of the Minamoto stockade fortress of Hiuchi in Echizen province, but Yoshinaka had been monitoring their movements, and inflicted a huge defeat upon the Taira at the battle of Kurikara (Tonamiyama). He first held the Taira in position by conducting an elaborate set-piece battle involving an archery duel and acts of individual combat. This was the ideal of armed conflict to which most samurai aspired, but Yoshinaka had an ulterior motive, because while this martial ceremonial was going on, a detachment of his army were working their way round to the Taira rear. To add to the surprise of their attack, the Minamoto tied lighted pine torches to the horns of a herd of

bulls, and stampeded them into the Taira ranks.

The defeat of the Taira expeditionary force enabled Yoshinaka to make a rapid advance on Kyoto, a move that caused as much alarm to his cousin Minamoto Yoritomo as it did to the Taira, and the next enemies that Yoshinaka had to deal with were from his own family. In 1184 Yoritomo sent an army under his brother Yoshitsune, who found his way to the capital blocked at Uji. Once again, the river was being used as a line of defense, but in this case the defense was from north to south. Yoshitsune's samurai, who had no doubt heard of the famous exploits from 1180, hoped to emulate these examples themselves, and a race began to become the first across the river. The accolade was won by Sasaki Takatsuna, who told his

Right: Minamoto Kiso Yoshinaka, depicted here on a painted scroll at the Gichuji in Otsu, where he is buried.

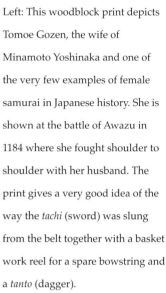

Left: This woodblock print depicts Tomoe Gozen, the wife of Minamoto Yoshinaka and one of the very few examples of female samurai in Japanese history. She is shown at the battle of Awazu in 1184 where she fought shoulder to shoulder with her husband. The print gives a very good idea of the way the *tachi* (sword) was slung from the belt together with a basket work reel for a spare bowstring and a *tanto* (dagger).

rival that his saddle girth was loose. While the other paused to adjust it, Sasaki rode to glory.

Beaten at Uji, Yoshinaka withdrew with his cousin in pursuit, and was apprehended at Awazu, where, together with his wife, the renowned female warrior Tomoe Gozen, he fought to the last. Yoshinaka was beheaded while his most loyal followers committed suicide. The main branch of the Minamoto could now concentrate on defeating their greatest enemies; the Taira.

A year of battles followed, all of which were led by Minamoto Yoshitsune on behalf of his elder brother Yoritomo, who stayed behind in Kamakura. Yoshitsune's first move was directed against the Taira fortress of Ichinotani, which was built on the edge of the sea beneath a steep cliff near to present day

Left: Sato Tadanobu, one of the loyal companions of Minamoto Yoshitsune, is shown here fighting for his master in the snow. He has discarded his bow in preference to his samurai sword. The way in which his arrows are tied inside his open basket-work quiver is clearly shown in this print.

Right: The celebrated feat by the archer Nasu Yoichi at the battle of Yashima in 1184, when he shot a fan from off the top of the mast of a Taira ship anchored offshore.

Kobe. While one detachment attacked along the shore, Yoshitsune led his samurai in a surprise cavalry charge down the steep slope to the rear of the stockade. Many celebrated acts of single combat then took place on the beach as the Taira escaped to their ships.

The great strength of the Taira had always been their seafaring skills and their command of the Inland Sea area. The new trump card they possessed was the child emperor Antoku, who was the grandson of the late Taira Kiyomori and the unquestionable proof of Taira legitimacy to rule. Only he could pronounce the Minamoto to be rebels against the throne. Their first refuge was Yashima on Shikoku island, but Yoshitsune pursued them thither, and defeated them again in another battle on a beach. This encounter was enlivened by the exploit of the archer Nasu Yoichi, who displayed his skill by shooting a fan from off the mast of one of the Taira ships.

It took many more months for the Minamoto to be able to challenge the Taira once again in their final redoubt, which was an island in the narrow Shimonoseki straits between the main Japanese islands of Honshu and Kyushu. Here took place the decisive sea battle of Dan no Ura in 1185, where the Minamoto beat the Taira at their own game. In one of the most decisive battles in Japanese history the Taira were annihilated. The child emperor was deliberately drowned so that he would not fall into the Minamoto's hands, and many dramatic suicides followed. The sea around ran red with the blood of the slain and the red dye from the Taira flags, and even the crabs that lived in the sea were said to be possessed by the ghosts of the dead samurai.

The Minamoto had won decisively, and Yoritomo moved east from Kamakura to claim his prize, but it was not long before he grew to look upon his heroic brother as a rival. Yoshitsune was therefore outlawed, and Yoritomo's men pursued him the length and breadth of Japan, finally catching up with him at the battle of Koromogawa in the far north of Japan in 1189. There Yoshitsune committed suicide, leaving his brother's position finally unchallenged. To consolidate his triumph Yoritomo made two important and far reaching decisions. The first was to have himself proclaimed shogun, the title originally given as a temporary commission to the general sent by the Nara court to quell the northern barbarians. Yoritomo made the institution of the shogunate a permanent one, and the post, now equivalent to a military dictator, was not relinquished until the emergence of modern Japan in the nineteenth century. His other decision was to abandon the imperial capital of Kyoto for a new capital in the Minamoto stronghold of Kamakura, far to the east. From now on the emperor would be little more than a figurehead. The creation of the shogunate meant that the samurai now ruled Japan.

The Shokyu War

In spite of the totality of their victory over the Taira, the Minamoto family did not have long to enjoy their triumph. There were only three Minamoto shoguns in all and, by 1219, their power had been eclipsed by the Hojo family. Although related by marriage to the Minamoto,

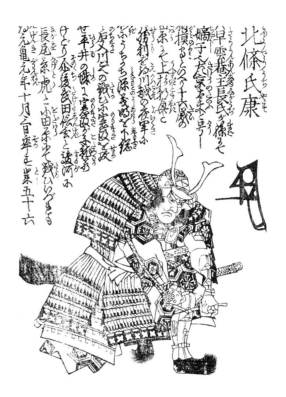

Left: Hojo Ujiyasu, the most successful of the five generations of the Hojo family.

their respect for the institution of shogun was such that they ruled with the title of regents.

The Hojo were challenged in their turn by Emperor Go-Toba, of the imperial family, who wished to restore the imperial throne to the position it had enjoyed before Yoritomo. Go-Toba began by denouncing Regent Hojo Yoshitoki as an outlaw. Three days later a further statement was made decreeing the whole of the eastern half of the country to be in a state of rebellion. Both announcements were designed to catch Kamakura unawares, but a relay of fast messengers had managed to warn Yoshitoki of the former proclamation by the day the latter was issued, and he immediately took steps to assure himself of the loyalty of neighboring samurai.

The Hojo's first consideration was one of defense, so they closed the passes of Ashigara

Right: The Tsurugaoka Hachiman Shrine in Kamakura, a place forever associated with the doomed members of the Minamoto shogunate.

and Hakone in the Mount Fuji area to prevent any advance on Kamakura from the west. But bolder spirits argued that attack would be the better response to the imperial forces, so a plan was drawn up involving a march on Kyoto. The imperial troops were largely inexperienced and had little will to fight the warriors from the east, whose fathers' reputations had preceded them. Many of the defenders fled from their positions and put their trust in the natural moat of the Uji River, so for the third time in half a century the bridge of Uji echoed to the din of war. This third battle of Uji lasted all day, but by nightfall the road to Kyoto was open. Hojo Yasutoki (Yoshitoki's eldest son) made a grand entrance on the following day and received the surrender of Go-Toba.

Thus ended the brief Shokyu Rebellion, so called from the era name of Shokyu (1219–1221). The Hojo's triumph was due largely to their boldness in advancing. Go-Toba was exiled and the regency confiscated the largest area of defeated enemies' lands since the fall of the Taira. Warrior rule of Japan had been dramatically confirmed.

The Mongol Invasions

A far more serious challenge to the Hojo, and to the samurai class in general, was made half a century later. The two attempts by Khublai Khan, the Yuan (Mongol) Emperor of China, to conquer Japan provide the first of only two illustrations from the whole of samurai warfare when the samurai were pitted against foreign enemies rather than their own kind. It is also the first occasion since the Nara period when the samurai fought for Japan itself, instead of some narrow factional or clan interest.

The first Mongol Invasion, which was carried out in 1274, was of such brief duration that it amounted to little more than a reconnaissance in force, a tactic which the Mongols had often used in their campaigns on the Asiatic mainland. Landfall was made in the sheltered Hakata Bay, where the modern city of Fukuoka now stands. Mongol detachments came ashore at various sites along the shore, and were met by the arrows of the samurai. The Mongols' advance and withdrawal to the accompaniment of drums, bells, and shouted war cries alarmed the Japanese horses. The samurai were also faced with a different archery technique,

whereby arrows were shot in huge clouds, rather than being used in long-range individual combat. Dense showers of arrows, some tipped with poison, were poured into the Japanese lines, and exploding bombs were thrown by catapult. During the night a fierce storm blew up which severely damaged the fleet lying at anchor, so the Mongols immediately set sail back to Korea to plan their next move.

Over the next few years the Japanese made defense preparations, including the building of a stone wall along the most vulnerable sections of the coast, and even considered a raid on the Korean seaboard, although this was never carried out. The resulting attack that made up the second invasion in 1281 was a much larger effort, and evidence suggests that the Mongols intended to establish a permanent outpost. The Mongols established themselves on two islands in Hakata bay, one of which, Shiga, was connected to the mainland by a narrow spit of land. From these islands they launched repeated attacks against the Japanese for about a week. The Japanese responded with night raids against the Mongol ships, and managed to prevent further landings, but Mongol reinforcements were on their way. Just when things were looking desperate for the Japanese attack, a typhoon blew up. This was the famous *kamikaze*, the wind of the gods. It wrecked the Mongol fleet, and few survivors made it back to the continent. The combination of divine assistance and samurai bravery ensured that the defeat of the Mongol invasions entered the most glorious annals of Japanese warfare.

Above: The wall built as a defense against a future Mongol invasion at Hakata Bay, Kyushu.

Above left: A samurai archer shoots a Mongol as the army pull back from the terrifying onslaught.

Right: The "Mongol mound" on the island of Shiga in Hakata Bay, erected by local Nichiren sect members as a memorial on the site where bodies of the Mongol warriors were washed ashore.

This twelfth-century samurai is now fully armored. We see the *tachi*, the famous samurai sword, worn cutting edge downward. It is suspended from the belt along with a basketwork disc holding a spare bowstring. His *yumi* (bow) is of composite construction, and tied round with rattan. His quiver is tied over his shoulder and hangs at his waist. The arrows were drawn out in a downward direction.

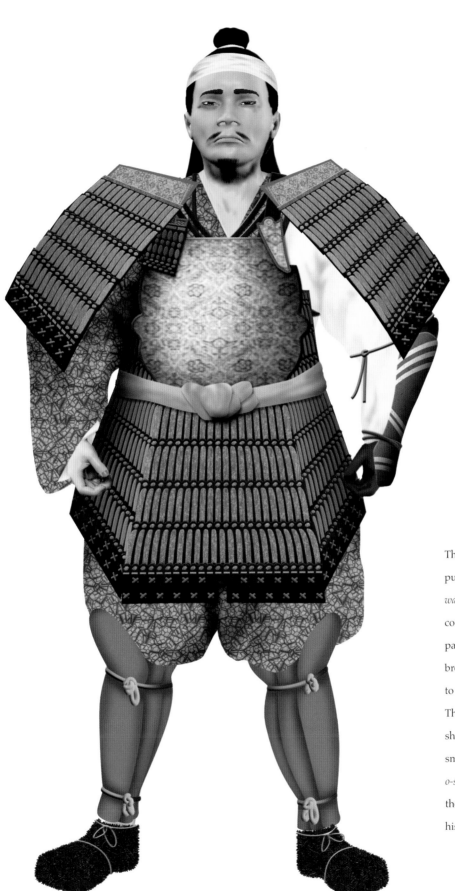

The rest of the *yoroi* has now been put on. It is made exactly like the *waidate* section, but the front of it is covered with a *tsurubashiri* (sheet of patterned leather). It looks like a breastplate but its main purpose is to allow ease of drawing the bow. The suspensory cords from the shoulders are protected by two small armor plates. Two very large *o-sode* (shoulder guards), typical of the age, protect the upper part of his arms.

Beneath the samurai's right arm hangs the first piece of armor plate. It is called the *waidate* and is the only separate section of the *yoroi* (armor). It is of lamellar construction, consisting of rows of overlapping metal or leather scales bound together and lacquered. A series of these horizontal sections are tied vertically with silk cords to make a strong but flexible armor plate.

On top of his undergarments the samurai has placed a very ornamental *yoroi-hitatare* (armor robe), which is a two-piece garment consisting of a jacket with long wide sleeves and separate trousers tucked into gaiters. Everything is tied in securely at the waist using a white *obi* (belt). We also see the first items of armor. On his legs are heavy iron *suneate* (shinguards) which come up to the knee. On his left arm he wears a *kote* (sleeve armor). He is not wearing one on his right arm because he will need the maximum freedom of movement to draw his bow. On his feet are boots made from bearskin.

The samurai has dressed his hair and has tied a white *hachimaki* (headband) round his forehead. He is wearing a white kimono, a garment similar to a dressing gown, over which he has put a pair of wide loose trousers. The trousers are tied at the waist.

本朝廿四孝

本間源内兵衛資忠

Right: Here we see a fine example of the self-sacrificing tradition of the samurai that dates from the Gempei Wars. The hero Suketada writes his name in blood on the pillar of a temple.

Left: The Daibutsudan, or Great Buddha Hall, of the Todaiji in Nara. This building houses the world's largest bronze statue, which is of Amida Buddha in a seated position. The city of Nara was burned down during the Gempei Wars, but all its temples were rebuilt.

The Nanbokucho Wars

In the early part of the fourteenth century, the Hojo regency faced another attempt at imperial restoration. Emperor Go-Daigo was brave and energetic, and chroniclers speak well of the reforms he introduced. Go-Daigo's energy contrasted with the lack of action the Hojo took against him. It was also very different from their speedy reaction to Go-Toba's similar attempts a century earlier. There was an equally sluggish reply when they received hard evidence that Go-Daigo was preparing to challenge their rule by force. When they eventually sent an army from Kamakura, Go-Daigo had full knowledge of their approach and sufficient time to plan accordingly, including the recruitment of warrior monks. Go-Daigo left Kyoto for the safety of the Todaiji in Nara, taking with

him the imperial regalia that were the symbols of his sovereignty. The Todaiji monks expressed concern that they could not withstand an attack by the Hojo, so Go-Daigo moved on to Kasagi, a mountain some 600-feet-high, overlooking the Kizugawa. It, too, was the home of warrior monks, who welcomed him and strengthened their position against an expected attack.

The Hojo first tried to negotiate, but when Go-Daigo refused to abdicate the drastic decision was made to raise another member of the imperial family to the throne instead. Go-Daigo had therefore been officially deposed, but he still had the regalia, so the actual enthronement ceremony had to be postponed until the items were recaptured, an effort that began immediately.

It is at this point in the war that we first hear the name of Kusunoki Masashige, a

Right: The view looking down from the site of the fortress of Chihaya, defended valiantly by Kusunoki Masashige.

warrior whose skill in warfare, and above all his loyalty to the legitimate emperor, was to make him the model of perfection for all samurai. Kusunoki Masashige fought for Go-Daigo from a *yamashiro* (mountain castle) called Akasaka, but his imperial loyalist army was short of troops and soon only the terrain frustrated the attackers' attempts. The castle fell in November 1331 but, instead of making a last-ditch stand and committing honorable suicide, Kusunoki Masashige and Go-Daigo's son Prince Morinaga both escaped to carry on the fight. However, on his way to join them in Akasaka, Go-Daigo had been captured and taken to the Hojo headquarters in Kyoto. A few months later, in 1332, he was exiled to the island of Oki. It appeared to all that Go-Daigo's revolt had been crushed as thoroughly as that of Go-Toba, and that resistance was useless.

Had it not been for Kusunoki Masashige

and Prince Morinaga, this latest attempt at imperial restoration would indeed have been over. Instead they established further positions in the mountains and held out against the Hojo, who launched a full-scale assault on Kusunoki's new fortifications at Chihaya. Chihaya was much stronger than Akasaka and a great army of the Hojo became practically immobilized in front of this makeshift mountain fortress. All of Kusunoki Masashige's skills were brought to bear in enticing the enemy to attack him in places where the terrain, with which Kusunoki's men were familiar, proved as much of a hindrance as the loyalists' arrows. Huge boulders were balanced on cliff edges, ready to be dislodged into passes full of Hojo soldiers, who were also tempted into night attacks and picked off at will. Pits were dug across paths, felled trees provided almost insurmountable obstacles and, with every day that they spent frustrated in the forests round Chihaya, more and more samurai clans were shown that Kamakura could be challenged, and were encouraged to try their hand.

Chihaya was never captured, and its continuing existence inspired the exiled Go-Daigo to return in the spring of 1333. He landed in Hoki province, on the Japan Sea coast west of Kyoto. The Hojo sent one of their leading generals against him. He was called Ashikaga Takauji, and soon realized what an opportunity had come his way. Unlike any other of Go-Daigo's other supporters, his Ashikaga family had the lineage which would enable them to accept the position of shogun from a captive, or even a merely grateful emperor. Takauji's future clearly lay with Go-Daigo, not the Hojo Regency, so Ashikaga Takauji turned away from a pursuit of Go-Daigo and launched his army against the Hojo's Kyoto headquarters at Rokuhara. The surprise element was total, and he succeeded in capturing the city for the rightful emperor. When the news of the victory reached the Hojo at Chihaya, the siege was abandoned and many of the samurai went over to the imperial camp.

The Hojo strength was now largely confined to eastern Japan, and its doom was almost complete when, in June 1333, a warrior called Nitta Yoshisada joined the imperial supporters. He collected other opportunistic clans about him in Kozuke Province and descended from the mountains on to the Hojo's capital of Kamakura. Nitta divided his army into three and the columns slowly forced their way through the narrow passes that acted as a natural defense for the city. Nitta then decided to outflank his enemy by a rapid march round the sea coast. Legend tells us that the tide was in, so Nitta prayed to Amaterasu, the goddess of the sun, and threw his sword into the sea as an offering, at which the waters retreated. This is how the *Taiheiki* tells it:

> He dismounted from his horse, stripped off his helmet, and fell down and worshipped the sea, praying to the dragon-gods with all his might. I have heard that the Sun-Goddess of Ise, the founder of the land of Japan, conceals her true being in the august image of Vairocana Buddha, and that she has appeared in this world in the guise of a dragon-god of the blue ocean. Now her descendant our Emperor drifts on the waves of the western seas, oppressed by rebellious subjects...Let the eight dragon-gods of the inner and outer seas look upon my loyalty; let them roll back the tides a myriad leagues distant to open a way for my hosts.
>
> So he prayed, and cast his gold-mounted sword into the sea. May it not be that the dragon-gods accepted it? At the setting of the moon that night, suddenly for more than 2,000 yards the waters ebbed away from Inamura Cape, where for the first time a broad flat beach appeared. Likewise, the thousands of warships deployed to shoot flanking arrows were carried away with the running tide, until they floated far out on the sea. How strange it was! Never was such a thing as this!

...the tide was in, so Nitta prayed to Amaterasu, the goddess of the sun, and threw his sword into the sea as an offering, at which the waters retreated.

Right: A view of the city of Kamakura, site of the last stand of the Hojo regents in the fierce battle of 1333.

Right: Ashikaga Yoshiaki, the last of the Ashikaga shoguns. He was deposed by Oda Nobunaga.

When Kamakura fell the Hojo rulers withdrew to a secluded spot and committed suicide.

The Ashikaga Shoguns

Throughout samurai history the achievement of personal glory and the provision of noble service always had a considerably mercenary dimension. Thus it was that when Ashikaga Takauji succeeded in putting Go-Daigo back on his throne he expected to be paid for it, and when the forthcoming reward was not sufficient, Ashikaga Takauji revolted. Unlike the Hojo, the Ashikaga family were of Minamoto stock, and thus could accept the commission of shogun. This made Ashikaga Takauji a particularly dangerous enemy, and Go-Daigo acted

swiftly to defeat Takauji's army and drive him away to the southern main island of Kyushu. But Takauji was not beaten, and having licked his wounds he raised troops in Kyushu, and by June 1336 his army was back again, advancing on Kyoto by sea and land.

The news soon reached the imperial court. Loyal as ever, Kusunoki Masashige recommended to Go-Daigo that he should take to the mountains again to fight a guerrilla campaign, but the emperor was against it. Instead he ordered Kusunoki to meet Ashikaga in battle. As an experienced soldier Kusunoki Masashige

realized that the course of action Go-Daigo was advocating was likely to prove disastrous, but it was not his place to disobey the commands of his emperor. Masashige therefore marched out of Kyoto and gave battle to Ashikaga at Minatogawa, the site of which is in present-day Kobe city. As expected, the loyalists were heavily defeated and so Kusunoki committed suicide. Kusunoki Masashige thus entered the pantheon of samurai heroes as the greatest exemplar of loyalty to the emperor.

The new shogun appointed an emperor of his own, and for the next half century Japan

Above: The Minatogawa Shrine within the modern city of Kobe marks the site of the great battle where Kusunoki Masashige was killed.

Right: Kusunoki Masashige's farewell to his son Masatsura is one of the most poignant tales in Japanese history. Masatsura promised to continue the struggle, and eventually met his death at the battle of Shijo-Nawate in 1348.

was to have two imperial lines, the legitimate "Southern Court" in Yoshino, and the "Northern Court," the Ashikaga nominees, in Kyoto. Much fighting took place between the rival supporters, who included in particular the successive generations of Kusunoki and Ashikaga family members. For example, Kusunoki Masashige's son Masatsura perished in the battle of Shijo-Nawate in 1348.

The rival imperial lines were finally reunited in 1392, thanks to the supreme diplomatic skills of the shogun Ashikaga Yoshimitsu, one of the greatest rulers in Japanese history. He was also an enthusiastic patron of the arts, and

was the builder of Kyoto's famous Kinkakuji (Golden Pavilion). Yet even after the imperials' schism had ended, occasional conflicts arose in the name of a supposedly legitimate emperor, although the main military concern of Yoshimitsu's reign was the need to quell the activities of the Japanese pirates who raided Korea and China.

On several occasions the Koreans hit back against the pirates. In 1380, 500 Japanese ships were set ablaze in the mouth of the Kum River. Korean ships now sported the contemporary world's finest cannon, and the fight was once actually taken to the Japanese during a raid on the pirates' lair of Tsushima island in 1389.

Among the devices designed to win the hearts and minds of those who had influence over the *wako* was the granting of official titles to cooperative *daimyo*. These were accompanied by appropriate stipends and the issue of copper seals, possession of which had the similar effect of legitimating trade that was enjoyed on a larger scale by the shogun through the tribute system. The family who benefited most from these arrangements were the So, whose territories lay closest to Korea. They were based on Tsushima, an island only thirty miles from the Korean shore, yet 150 miles from the Japanese mainland. Tsushima had been the first place to be attacked during the Mongol invasions in 1274 and 1281, an action in which the So's ancestors had participated most heroically. The island was also a pirates' lair, but in response to entreaties from the Choson court the *daimyo* of Tsushima concluded the so-called Kakitsu Treaty with Korea in 1443. Not only were the So allowed to sponsor fifty vessels a year for the Korea trade, they were also given the responsibility of overseeing every Japanese ship that went to Korea, a checkpoint system that proved to be highly lucrative for them. In 1461, So Shigetomo asked for and received the investiture by the Korean court of the title of governor of Tsushima, an honor that further served to increase the So's own feelings of self-importance, and helped to persuade the Koreans that Tsushima was actually part of their country.

Left: The Kinkakuji or Golden Pavilion, the greatest artistic achievement of the reign of the shogun Ashikaga Yoshimitsu.

CHAPTER 2

the age of the samurai

A quarrel between two samurai houses developed into a military and political disaster.

Right: Toyotomi Hideyoshi blows the conch shell to order the attack at the battle of Shizugatake in 1583.

Opposite page: The Ginkakuji or Silver Pavilion, built by Ashikaga Yoshimasa to emulate his grandfather, the builder of the Golden Pavilion. Unfortunately the money ran out before it could be covered in silver leaf.

The Onin War

The first half of the fifteenth century in Japan saw sporadic rebellions taking place, all of which were quelled successfully until 1467, when a quarrel between two samurai houses developed into a military and political disaster. The resulting Onin War was fought largely around the capital and even in the streets of Kyoto itself, which was soon reduced to a smoking wasteland. The shogun at the time was Ashikaga Yoshimasa, Yoshimitsu's grandson, who was totally unable to prevent a slide into anarchy. Instead Yoshimasa contented himself with artistic pursuits, and was one of the early devotees of the tea ceremony. He also built the Ginkakuji (Silver Pavilion) in an attempt to emulate his illustrious ancestor. His cultural achievements were many, but the power of the shogunate declined as never before.

With such a vacuum at the heart of Japanese politics, many samurai took the opportunity to develop their own local autonomy in a way that had not been seen for centuries. It was as if the powerful landowners of the Nara period had been reborn, and throughout Japan there was a scramble for territory. Some ancient families disappeared altogether to be replaced by men who had once fought for them and achieved local power through war, intrigue, marriage, or murder. Other ancient lines prospered, and found themselves having to share Japan with upstarts who may have started their careers as *ashigaru* (foot soldiers) but who now owned a considerable amount of territory, which they

defended using wooden castles and loyal followers. These lords called themselves *daimyo* (great names), and led lives that were constantly being challenged by neighbors. Literally scores of battles took place, leading to the century and a half between 1467 and 1600 being dubbed the *Sengoku Jidai* (the period of Warring States), by analogy with a similar turbulent period in ancient China.

A good example of the trend was to be found in north-central Japan where the territories of the Takeda and Uesugi families were located. They were at war for half a century. Their most famous members, Takeda Shingen and Uesugi Kenshin, were princes in their own provinces, and led thousands of fanatically loyal samurai. Takeda Shingen is customarily credited with being the finest leader of mounted samurai in Sengoku Japan. At Uedahara in 1548 and at Mikata ga Hara in 1572, the Takeda cavalry rode down disorganized infantry missile units. But for cavalry charges to succeed, the old samurai tradition of singling out a worthy opponent for a challenge to single combat had to wait until the enemy line was broken, so group operations became the norm.

The Takeda and Uesugi fought each other five times at a place called Kawanakajima ("the island within the river"), a battlefield that marked the border between their territories. Not only were the armies the same, the same two commanders led them at each battle. In addition to this intriguing notion of five battles on one battlefield, Kawanakajima has also become the epitome of Japanese chivalry and romance: the archetypal clash of samurai arms.

The Onin War was fought largely around the capital and even in the streets of Kyoto itself, which was soon reduced to a smoking wasteland.

In its more extreme form, this view even denies the possibility that anyone actually got hurt at the Kawanakajima battles, which are seen only as a series of "friendly fixtures" characterized by posturing and pomp. In this scenario the Kawanakajima conflicts may be dismissed as mock warfare. During some of the encounters, admittedly, the two armies disengaged before committing themselves fully to a fight to the death, but the wounds and the dead bodies were real enough, and the fourth battle of Kawanakajima in 1561 produced many casualties on both sides.

There was still a shogun in Kyoto while such wars were going on, but his existence was of little consequence except for providing the legitimation for a potential power struggle. This could possibly lead to a coup similar to that which had led the Hojo to overthrow the last Minamoto shogun in 1219. But to succeed in such a scheme a *daimyo* had to take Kyoto, and

if any of them was rash enough to try and march on the capital, he could almost guarantee that one of his local rivals would rush to attack his province and try to take possession of the territory he had left lightly defended.

It was not until 1560 that any *daimyo* felt sufficiently secure to risk such a move. One lord called Imagawa Yoshimoto, however, had a huge army, and was based on the Pacific Coast road which gave him excellent communications toward Kyoto. The only obstacle in his way was Owari province, the territory of a comparatively minor *daimyo* called Oda Nobunaga, whose army Imagawa outnumbered by a factor of 12 to one. The advance began with the capture of Nobunaga's border castles, which Imagawa celebrated in some style with the customary head inspection

Below: The memorial statue depicting the famous single combat between Uesugi Kenshin and Takeda Shingen at the fourth battle of Kawanakajima in 1561.

ceremony in a little valley called Okehazama. His success had made him careless, and Oda Nobunaga took advantage of the situation to launch a surprise attack under the cover of a thunderstorm. Imagawa Yoshimoto at first thought a brawl had broken out among his own troops, but no sooner did he realize what was actually happening than his head was off his shoulders. Young Oda Nobunaga had achieved one of the least expected victories in Japanese history.

As had happened so often in Japanese history, success bred success, and Oda Nobunaga soon found other samurai families only too eager to ally themselves with him. This gave him the opportunity to carry out his own march on Kyoto, where he deposed the current shogun in 1568 and gave himself powers of regency. There were many challenges to his impertinence, but in battles such as Anegawa (1570) Nobunaga defeated all his rivals, and his victory over the mighty Takeda at Nagashino in 1575 sealed his reputation as a military genius. Setting to one side the traditional samurai contempt for and mistrust of foot soldiers, Nobunaga trained his *ashigaru* to fire arquebuses in controlled volleys. This broke the charge of the renowned Takeda cavalrymen, and, even though the battle of Nagashino lasted another seven hours, a new trend had been set in samurai warfare.

Oda Nobunaga also encouraged trade with the newly arrived European merchants, their supplies of guns being their most highly valued commodity. But even Nobunaga's superlative battlefield skills could not save him from falling

victim to an assassination attempt and, in 1582, he and his bodyguard were suddenly overwhelmed by one of his own generals, Akechi Mitsuhide.

Nobunaga's ablest general, Toyotomi Hideyoshi, was campaigning many miles away when the coup happened. On hearing the awful news, Hideyoshi rushed back to Kyoto and defeated the usurper at the battle of Yamazaki. As Nobunaga's avenger, Hideyoshi felt that he had the right to inherit his late master's empire. Nobunaga's own family naturally objected, and once again the matter was resolved by force. In a furious year of sieges, marches, and battles such as Shizugatake (1583), Hideyoshi swept all local opposition to one side, and by 1585 he felt both confident and strong enough to extend

Right: In the aftermath of the battle of Yamazaki in 1582, the defeated general Akechi Mitsuhide is spotted by a vigilant peasant and killed.

Nobunaga's former territories still further. Invasions of Japan's other main islands of Shikoku and Kyushu followed, and with the submission of the northern *daimyo* in 1591, Japan was reunited once again—under the sword of a man who had started his military career as one of Nobunaga's foot soldiers.

Defining a Samurai

Prior to the time of Toyotomi Hideyoshi, the definition of who was and was not a samurai was a very loose one, to which no general paid much attention. Leaders such as Takeda Shingen commanded armies that were very "professional" in their outlook and their operations, but they often had only a small core of men who might be termed "regular soldiers." These warriors might be family members or hereditary retainers, and were often outnumbered by part-time soldiers who would fight for some of the year and do agricultural work the rest of the time. The troops of the Chosokabe Motochika of Shikoku island were well-known

Above: Young Toyotomi Hideyoshi, with his armor stacked neatly behind him, makes his farewells to his aged mother before setting off on a military career.

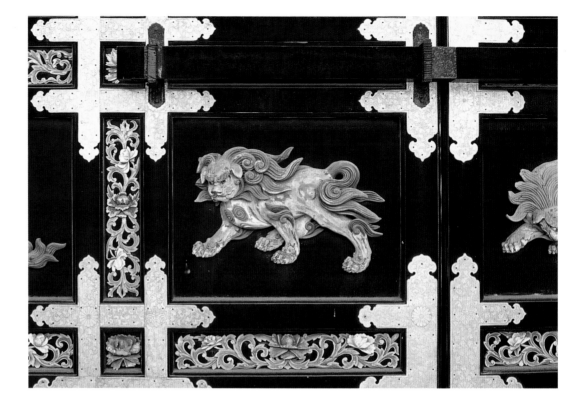

Right: The attractive detail to be found on the doors of the Nishi Honganji in Kyoto. These buildings were formerly part of Toyotomi Hideyoshi's palace, and are representative examples of Momoyama styles and taste.

in this regard, and were said to do agricultural work in the paddy fields with their sandals attached to the shafts of their spears that were thrust into the ground, ready to be used at a moment's notice.

Part-time soldiering was a very common feature in the period of Warring States. Many otherwise senior officers in a *daimyo*'s army still clung to their roots in the soil, and none of their masters had any desire to separate them from it. Their local economic success was often heavily dependent upon these part-time farmers, in just the same way as their military success was dependent on part-time soldiers who were happy to be rewarded with grants of land for their services. The successful *daimyo* was one who could balance these two vital functions.

This state of affairs began to change from about 1570 onward. One very important factor was the introduction of new weapons for the *ashigaru*. The first was the long spear, which sometimes reached the dimensions of the European pike. To put such a weapon into untrained hands was asking for trouble. Even though the Japanese spear was never wielded with the rigidity of formation of the legendary pike men of Switzerland, some form of "pike drill" was a necessity. Guns, too, could be a hindrance in untrained hands, but Oda Nobunaga's famous victory at Nagashino in 1575—when 3,000 arquebuses brought down the mounted samurai of the Takeda—made a point. Guns were clumsy and inefficient things, but when issued to trained and disciplined squads they produced devastating results.

This fifteenth-century samurai's *kabuto* (helmet) has a wide-flowing *shikoro* (brim) to ward off sword strokes. It is tied securely under his chin. He has a *tachi* (sword) suspended from his belt and two *tanto* (daggers) but his main weapon is a menacing-looking iron club, studded with rivets.

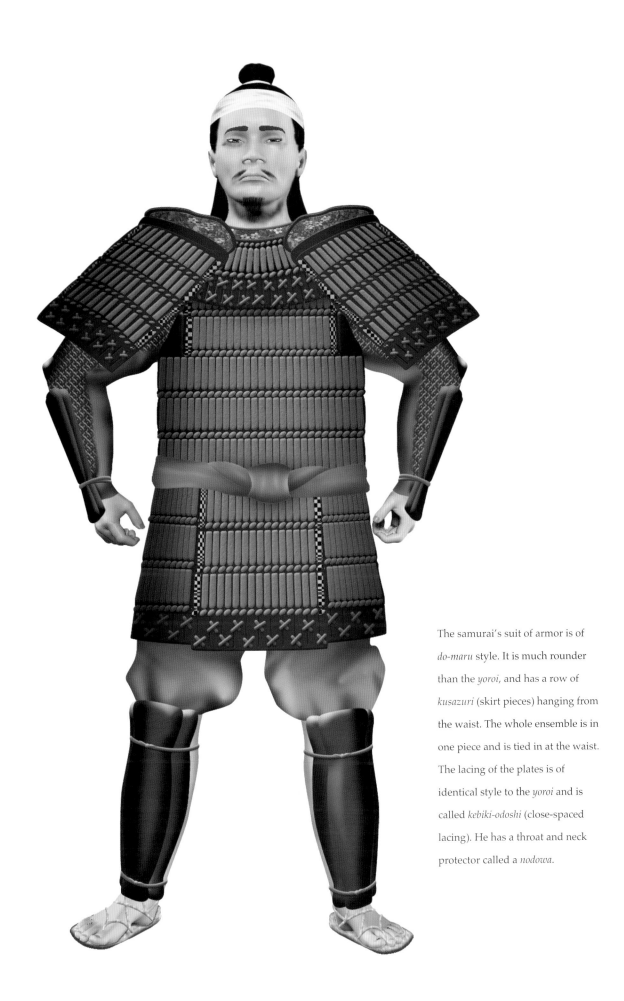

The samurai's suit of armor is of *do-maru* style. It is much rounder than the *yoroi*, and has a row of *kusazuri* (skirt pieces) hanging from the waist. The whole ensemble is in one piece and is tied in at the waist. The lacing of the plates is of identical style to the *yoroi* and is called *kebiki-odoshi* (close-spaced lacing). He has a throat and neck protector called a *nodowa*.

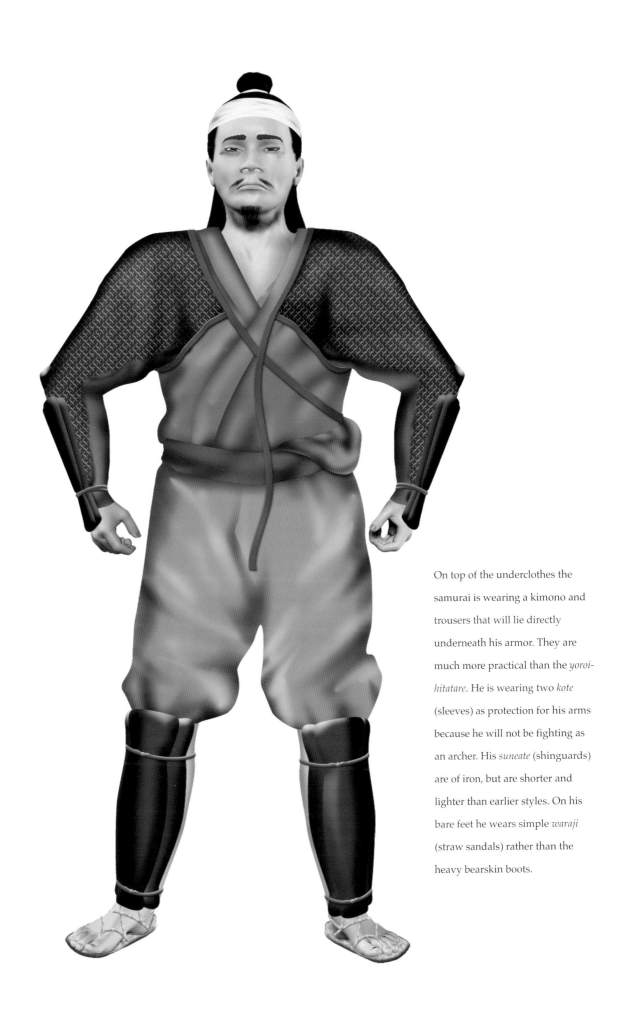

On top of the underclothes the samurai is wearing a kimono and trousers that will lie directly underneath his armor. They are much more practical than the *yoroi-hitatare*. He is wearing two *kote* (sleeves) as protection for his arms because he will not be fighting as an archer. His *suneate* (shinguards) are of iron, but are shorter and lighter than earlier styles. On his bare feet he wears simple *waraji* (straw sandals) rather than the heavy bearskin boots.

The samurai has added a set of underclothes. They are similar to the ones shown in the previous plate but are much simpler. The trousers are also short.

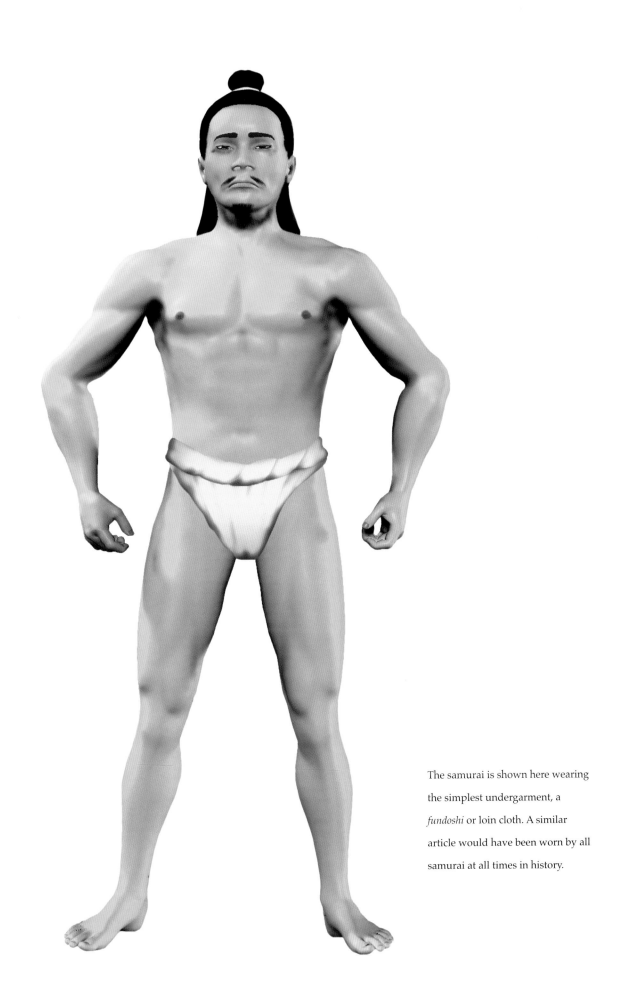

The samurai is shown here wearing the simplest undergarment, a *fundoshi* or loin cloth. A similar article would have been worn by all samurai at all times in history.

the battlefield. So the process that had been going on for half a century whereby stronger *daimyo* absorbed the territories of weaker ones began to accelerate, until with the triumph of Toyotomi Hideyoshi the system reached its logical conclusion.

In 1588 Hideyoshi enacted the first of two ordinances that were to have a huge influence on the definition of a samurai. The first was the famous "Sword Hunt," by which all weapons were to be confiscated from the peasantry and placed in the hands of the *daimyo* and their increasingly professional armies. By this act the means of making war were forcibly removed from anyone of whom Hideyoshi did not approve, because the Sword Hunt was much more than a search of farmers' premises. Minor *daimyo* whose loyalty was suspect, religious institutions who had the capacity for armed rebellion, and recalcitrant village headmen were all purged in an operation that has parallels with Henry VIII's dissolution of the monasteries.

The victims were told that the swords, spears, and guns thus collected would not be wasted, but would be melted down to make nails for the enormous image of Buddha that Hideyoshi was erecting in Kyoto. The nation would therefore benefit from the operation in two ways. It would be spiritually blessed, and would be freed from the curses of war and rebellion which had caused such disruption and suffering in the past. It is, however, more than likely that the majority of the weapons seized were not actually destroyed but stored ready for future campaigns.

Above: Torii Sune'emon, the hero of the siege of Nagashino in 1575. Sune'emon escaped from the beleaguered castle to request help. The subsequent response by Oda Nobunaga led to the famous battle of Nagashino.

The overall effect was to encourage training, discipline, and weapon specialization, and the time required to bring about all three inevitably cut into the rhythm of the agricultural year. For some *daimyo* balancing the equation proved impossible. Others, chiefly those with larger manpower resources to rely on, solved it through a division of labor between farmer and fighters, and it was the *daimyo* who chose this way that survived and prospered. The successful *daimyo* could field a larger and better-trained army, and the use of these larger and better-trained armies brought more success on

The Separation Edict which followed in 1591 completed the process. The peasants had been disarmed, and there was now to be a total separation between the military function and the productive (i.e. agricultural) function. No samurai was to be a farmer, and no farmer was to behave as a samurai. The Separation Edict therefore defined a distinction between samurai and farmer that was to continue throughout the Tokugawa period, the long time of peace that followed. It also allowed the potential for a reign of terror to be inflicted upon any local population who did not comply with Hideyoshi's wishes, a situation that was to apply almost immediately with the forced recruitment of peasants and fishermen for the invasion of Korea which Hideyoshi launched in 1592. Yet the Separation Edict had changed the nature of such recruitment for ever. No longer could a peasant like Hideyoshi enlist as an *ashigaru* and rise to be a general. From now on a peasant who was forced (or even volunteered) to do his duty would not carry out that function with a sword or gun in his hand, but with a cripplingly heavy pack on his back.

The Korean War

The war in Korea between 1592 and 1598 was a military fiasco that caused great suffering to many innocent people and damaged the economies of three countries, as Ming China was also drawn into the conflict along with Japan and Korea. During the initial invasion, the samurai carried all before them, and raced up the peninsula to capture Seoul within 20 days of their landing. Pusan, the main port, had been the first to fall, after a furious assault accompanied by utter savagery against the civilian population. In command of the garrison was Chong Pal. Refusing to surrender, he

Above: The Shimazu clan at the battle of Sach'on during the Korea War, 1598.

ordered his men to fight to the death, but was shot dead during the assault. A Japanese chronicler recorded that the samurai had even cut off the heads of dogs and cats in their intense fury.

The Korean generals sent from Seoul to oppose the invaders were confused and badly supported. At the battle of Sangju, General Yi Il was defeated and driven back toward the safety of a strategic pass, only to find to his horror that it had been abandoned. His colleague Sin Rip had decided to meet the Japanese in a cavalry battle in the plain to the north beside Ch'ungju, the most important fortress on the road to Seoul, where he drew up his forces with his back to two streams and flanked by rice paddies. Here he hoped the flat plain would give his cavalry the opportunity to sweep the Japanese away, but when he found that he was being slowly encircled he turned his horse into the river and killed himself. Many others did the same, and as the Japanese pressed forward the rest of the Korean army ran away. Seeing their army defeated the garrison of Ch'ungju surrendered, leaving Seoul open for occupation.

The Japanese advance then slowed down. They were delayed for a month at the Imjin River, and then again at the Taedong. This river guarded P'yongyang, which the Japanese took when a night attack by the Korean army disclosed the location of the fords. The first attempt to retake P'yongyang was launched by a Chinese army who crossed into Korea from the north. A much larger Chinese force laid siege to Py'ongyang in January 1593, and the sheer weight of numbers forced the Japanese army to withdraw back within the walls. Faced

with almost certain defeat, Konishi Yukinaga secretly evacuated the city during the night and retreated south with his army toward Seoul.

The ensuing battle of Pyokje was the largest conflict of the first invasion. It began as a rearguard action by Kobayakawa Takakage to allow the Japanese army to regroup in Seoul, which lay a short distance to the south. The Japanese counterattacked a largely Chinese army, and the fighting developed into a huge melee. In spite of having gained the victory, the morale of the Japanese army remained low, and instead of taking the offensive they now had their hands full with the defense of Seoul.

For the first 10 days of February 1593, Kwon Yul, who was perhaps the ablest of all the Korean generals, prepared to make a stand at Haengju. This was a fortress downstream on

Right: Konishi Yukinaga, who led the First Division during the Japanese invasion of Korea in 1592. This statue stands on the site of his castle of Uto.

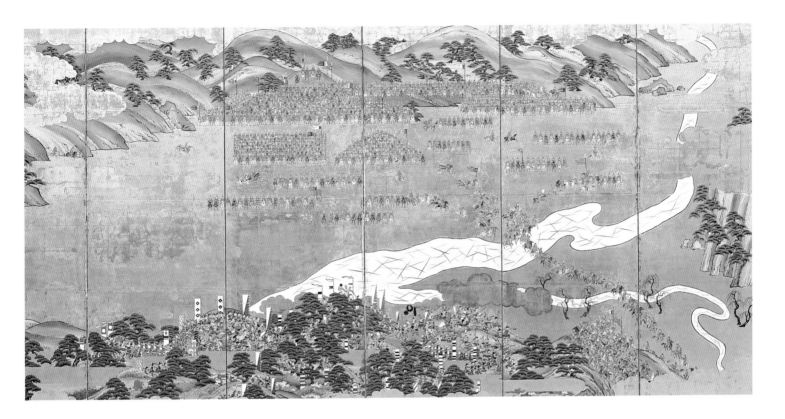

the Han River to the west of Seoul on a low hill, with the river as its southern defense. The resistance was desperate. Arrows were fired from *hwach'a* (multiple arrow launchers), and even women took part, carrying stones for throwing in their aprons tied round their waists. When the Japanese army launched a full attack, a fierce hand-to-hand fight began. Although the fight ebbed and flowed, the Japanese were faced with a relieving army of Koreans, so they retreated.

Korean guerrilla armies also played a vital role in the resistance against Japan. Under such leaders as the red-coated Kwak Chae-u they harassed Japanese forts and supply lines and fired delayed action mortar bombs among the Japanese garrisons. In August 1592, the Japanese garrison at Ch'ongju were beaten by a

guerilla army which consisted not only of Korean peasants, but Buddhist monks. The Korean monks were fierce fighters and skilled archers, and made up a sizeable proportion of Korea's irregular forces. At nearby Kumsan, in spite of defeating an army of 700 Koreans, known as the "Seven Hundred Brave Men," the Japanese general Kobayakawa Takakage was forced to retreat.

Guerrillas also took part in the first siege of Chinju Castle. Inside the fortress were 3,800 Korean soldiers and many civilian refugees. An assault on the walls began the following day, and continued into the night. The Japanese bombarded the walls with cannon and lit signal beacons outside the walls to intimidate the garrison. However, that same night a Korean guerrilla army approached the Japanese lines

Above: A huge Chinese army gathers to attack Ulsan castle, defended by the Japanese invaders, in Korea in 1597.

Right: Fighting in the snow, a lone swordsman triumphs over his victim.

from the rear, which greatly encouraged the defenders. Meanwhile the Japanese built a high tower from which they could fire down into the castle and brought up a thousand bamboo scaling ladders, to which the Korean soldiers and civilians responded with rocks and boiling water. That night 2,000 guerrillas managed to enter the castle while creating a diversion elsewhere. The Japanese army temporarily suspended the attack, but being faced with more guerrillas at their rear the assault was called off permanently.

The most decisive reverse for the Japanese occurred at sea. Korea's greatest hero and finest leader was Admiral Yi Sun-sin, who used a covered battleship called a turtle ship from the battle of Sach'on (1592) onward. Yi's most decisive victory was at Hansando. The straits allowed little space for maneuver, so Yi resolved to draw the Japanese out to a wider expanse of sea, which was in the vicinity of Hansando (Hansan island). This maneuver was successful, so the Japanese followed the lead set by Yi's scouting vessels, and as they approached Hansando found themselves sailing into the open arms of Yi's "crane formation." Yi's diary records the details of the epic struggle:

> Greatly encouraged by the initial victory, all the generals, officers and men stormed the enemy. They fired all the guns and arrows in their possession to burn the ships and kill all men of the hostile fleet. Annihilation was complete within a matter of hours.

In all, 47 Japanese ships were destroyed and 12 captured while 400 survivors swam ashore to Hansando. Because of this defeat the Japanese commanders lost control of the sea, and the first invasion was virtually over.

In spite of such a reversal Hideyoshi was determined to try again, and a second Japanese invasion of Korea was launched in 1597. Their first target, the castle of Namwon, held out against the enormous odds of the Japanese army for four days, but after much fierce fighting the invaders secured the approach to the moat. That night they began to pile bundles of green rice stalks up against a high, and thus lightly guarded, section of the wall. By the time the garrison realized what was happening the samurai were climbing up scaling ladders and pouring into the castle.

Yet once again the advancing Japanese were to be stopped in their tracks, this time at the indecisive battle of Chiksan, and they withdrew to their coastal fortresses. One of these castles, Ulsan, was then attacked by a huge Korean and Chinese army. The Japanese garrison was reduced to 5,000 men, who began to suffer from hunger and thirst as all access to water was cut off. At night foragers were sent out for water but often found the

Below: The Korean War dealt a severe blow to the power of the samurai clans and paved the way for the peaceful Tokugawa period. Few incidents ruffled the surface, but this is the most famous: The Loyal Retainers of Ako. Their leader Oishi Kuranosuke's statue now stands at the Sengakuji temple in Tokyo, where they are buried.

ponds filled with corpses. Soon the provisions were exhausted, and the troops were reduced to eating paper and even boiling the earth taken off the walls for meals. A few brave foragers ventured to go out during the night in search of bags of rice that could be found around the waists of some dead soldiers among the attackers. At the other end of the coastal defense line the castle of Sach'on was besieged. The Chinese and Koreans were driven off, but news soon arrived that Hideyoshi was dead, so the Japanese abandoned Korea for good.

Right: The castle of Okazaki, headquarters of Tokugawa Ieyasu.

The Tokugawa Peace

The great dictator Toyotomi Hideyoshi had ruled the whole of Japan, but he died leaving a five-year-old son to inherit his domains. Once again civil war broke out, coming to a climax in the decisive battle of Sekigahara in 1600. Sekigahara was fought between a coalition of *daimyo* loyal to Hideyoshi's son and Tokugawa Ieyasu. It was a battle that began with the dawn and continued in thick fog, and resulted in a victory for Ieyasu. But his success was by no means guaranteed. The battle hung in the balance for most of the day, and was only secured when the *daimyo* Kobayakawa Hideaki changed sides and joined the Tokugawa.

For Tokugawa Ieyasu the victory brought an almost unique reward. He was of Minamoto descent, so could legitimately become shogun. This he did in 1603. The Tokugawa then began a process to complete the social and legal separation of the samurai class by a physical separation. *Ashigaru* (foot soldiers) were firmly defined as the lowest ranks of the samurai class. All the samurai lived in the barracks of the castle town, while the farmers lived on the land and grew food. In theory it was a perfect system. The samurai owed loyalty and service to their *daimyo*, and all the *daimyo*, whose territories had either been extended, relocated, or diminished according to which side they had been on at Sekigahara, owed allegiance to the shogun.

Yet there were thousands who did not fit into the system, because the great civil wars that had raged in Japan had created an ever-increasing pool of unemployed samurai. Contrary to popular belief, Japanese battles rarely ended with either mass slaughter or multiple acts of suicide. Quite often a defeated *daimyo* was reinvested into his territories in return for a pledge of loyalty to the victor, such as happened with the absorption of the Sanada by the Takeda, but sometimes this proved impossible. Politics often meant that no accommodation could be reached with a victim. With

a lord both defeated and dead, and his followers labeled as rebels, the samurai who found
themselves on the losing side had lost almost
everything they had lived for or been trained
for. These were the men who became known as
ronin, "men of the waves," immortalized for
ever in Kurosawa's famous film *Seven
Samurai*, whose band of heroes are themselves
ronin. In the movie they are employed as hired
swords by a village. In real life they would
have been more likely to join another *daimyo*'s
army, because an ambitious warlord needed
every samurai he could get his hands on.

The doors of opportunity began to close for
ronin from the time of Sekigahara onward. All
daimyo were now theoretically in the service of
the shogun, and after all, wars had now supposedly ceased. Their landholdings were
known, down to the exact amount of rice they
produced and their army numbers were carefully monitored. There was therefore little
opportunity for casual recruitment, particularly
for a samurai whose lord had been on the losing side at Sekigahara. The result was that early
Tokugawa Japan had many *ronin* wandering its
byways, and these men could provide a
useful military resource for any rebel against
the Tokugawa.

The great chance for the *ronin* came in 1614.
Toyotomi Hideyori, the son of Japan's unifier
Hideyoshi, had been effectively usurped by
Tokugawa Ieyasu's triumph at Sekigahara. On
hearing rumors that the Tokugawa meant to
eliminate him, Hideyori packed his late father's
castle of Osaka with tens of thousands of rebel
ronin in a dramatic challenge to the Tokugawa

hegemony. Most of his followers were men who
had been dispossessed or had otherwise suffered from the Tokugawa takeover. The long
and bloody siege of Osaka was the result. The

Above: Toyotomi Hideyoshi, the
unifier of Japan.

It was over 20 years before another rebellion involving ronin *disturbed the calm of the "Tokugawa Peace."*

Right: Two foot soldiers stand guard over the crucifixion of Christian prisoners. The persecution of Christians was a dark side to the unification of Japan.

so-called winter campaign involved artillery bombardment and naval battles in the rivers that made up Osaka's moats. A peace settlement was drawn up that involved demolishing much of Osaka's outer defense works. Once the walls were down the Tokugawa returned. The siege ended with a huge and bloody battle at Tennoji in July 1615. The operation had lasted a year, and when it was over the heads of thousands of *ronin* were to be seen displayed on poles for miles around between Osaka and Kyoto.

The reign of the Tokugawa family appeared to have been finally secured. In fact it was over 20 years before another rebellion involving *ronin* disturbed the calm of the "Tokugawa Peace," but it did so only for a very short time. The Shimabara Rebellion of 1637–1638 had its origins in the monstrous behavior of the *daimyo* Matsukura Shigemasa, whose techniques for squeezing taxes out of his peasant farmers including tying them inside straw raincoats and setting the straw alight. The Shimabara peninsula was also a center of Christianity, a religion that had been banned by the shogun because of fears rising from its links to Europe. From being originally a peasants' revolt, the uprising rapidly grew into a religious war, with a degree of fanaticism that even the Osaka campaign had never matched. Once again hundreds of *ronin* joined a rebel army in taking on the Tokugawa, and once again they lost, but only after holding off the professional army of the shogun for many bitter and expensive months.

The Shimabara Rebellion proved to be the only serious challenge to the Tokugawa for the

Left: The site of the headquarters of the defeated general Ishida Mitsunari at the battle of Sekigahara in 1600.

next 200 years. Samurai were now the standing armies of the *daimyo*, who were now vassals of the shogun, and there were no battles left to fight. The samurai had to learn to cope with this new situation in a variety of ways.

The Wandering Swordsmen

The unemployed *ronin* found themselves in that isolated position through no fault of their own. A few samurai, however, chose not to stay within the system of feudal obligation to the shogun, and made their own decision to be independent. These were the men who were to achieve legendary status as the "wandering swordsmen" of Japan. By and large, their swords were not up for hire. Instead they traveled the country on *musha shugyo* (warrior pilgrimages), challenging other samurai to fight

Right: Miyamoto Musashi looks very formidable in this picture.

Below: The young Miyamoto Musashi is mocked by his more sophisticated colleagues as he displays a lack of table manners—evidence of his simple upbringing.

them almost to the death and seeking Zen enlightenment as they did so. None is better known than the famous Miyamoto Musashi, whose many duels with rivals have provided the material for endless plays, books, and movies. Musashi was an expert at pulling the blow from his sword, and his skill was said to include severing a rice grain placed on an opponent's forehead without cutting the man's skin. He usually fought with wooden swords, where bruises were all that the defeated man had to complain about.

Some of the legendary wanderers did settle down eventually and became retained samurai

in the service of a *daimyo*. The Yagyu, for example, became the teachers of swordsmanship to the shogun's family. Others entered monasteries, while some swordsmen were also literary men who composed books that sought a spiritual dimension to the way of the sword. Many of these, such as Miyamoto Musashi's *Book of Five Rings* are classics of samurai literature. Others sought more mundane employment as *yojimbo* (bodyguards), and were sometimes employed by the criminal gangs who controlled the gambling dens of the time.

Samurai Mercenaries

The most interesting, and least well-known activities of the samurai of the Tokugawa period were the exploits of those who went off to seek their fortunes overseas. Some were involved in trade, either legitimately as merchants or illegally as pirates. Others went openly as mercenaries, but in nearly all cases their swords were kept ready for use. In one dramatic incident a group of Japanese samurai in Taiwan were involved in an uprising that led to the overthrow of the Dutch governor, while the mercenaries employed by the King of Siam played an important role in Siamese politics.

Left: The swordsman Miyamoto Musashi in intense mood. He is extremely alert, and he appears to be making mystical *mudra* signs with his fingers.

Below: A demonstration of how to overcome a swordsman using a move of *jujitsu*.

Right: Ikeda Terumasa (1564–1613), whose life spanned the most glorious age of the samurai.

Mercenary warfare was a new concept, because mercenary in its European meaning was virtually unknown in Japan itself. There were no Japanese *condottieri* (the notorious Italian mercenary captains), and no equivalent of the specialist weapons units for hire like the Genoese crossbowmen. The nearest parallel was the hiring of the famous *ninja,* in which Iga province had a valued specialty. Yet from the late sixteenth century onward we can identify references to Japanese samurai fighting in foreign armies. The most important country was Siam (Thailand), where Japanese warriors provided a bodyguard for the King and were highly valued. A Dutchman called Van Vliet wrote that the Japanese "are the best soldiers and have always been highly esteemed by the various kings for their bravery. The greater number of the soldiers are cowardly Siamese."

The earliest reference to Japanese fighting for Siam occurs in 1579 in a Siamese source, but this is unfortunately not confirmed by any Japanese record. It refers to a company of 500 Japanese mercenaries helping the Siamese during the invasion by Burma and Laos. The men may have been taken to Siam by Portuguese ships, but it is strange that no names or locations are known. King Naresuen of Siam was very active in Asian politics during his reign, which coincided with Hideyoshi's invasion of Korea in 1592, and actually offered to China the use of the Siamese navy to fight the Japanese fleet, a gesture that was politely declined.

It is not until 1606 that we have written records of intercourse between Japan and Siam, and in the numerous letters that passed to and fro, military matters appear frequently. Tokugawa Ieyasu had been assured by his military advisors that Siamese gunpowder was of very good quality, so this became an important trading commodity. The legendary Japanese swords were equally valued in Siam, as were Japanese horses, which is somewhat surprising in view of how poorly they were regarded everywhere else.

Not all trading activity was this open or even legitimate. During the fourteenth and fifteenth centuries, piracy had been one of the main means by which Japan had conducted its relations with foreign countries. As Japanese maritime activities increased during the first few years of the seventeenth century, piracy again reared its ugly head. The inhabitants of the coasts of Siam, Cambodia, and Vietnam soon became as wary of Japanese pirates as the Koreans had been of them over a century earlier. When the King of Cambodia wrote to complain to Tokugawa Ieyasu, the shogun replied that he had his full support to punish them according to the laws of Cambodia.

Other countries also became involved. In December 1605, a certain John Davis became the first Englishman ever to be killed by a Japanese when his ship was involved in a fight with Japanese pirates off the Siamese coast. In 1614, men of the East India Company killed eight Japanese in a skirmish at Ayuthia, the Siamese capital. In 1616, Richard Cocks' diary records an alarming incident that was reported to him from Ayuthia by a Mr. Matthias, a Dutchman. An English trader called Mr. Pitts had an argument with a certain James Peterson, and he employed three samurai to assault his rival!

Cambodia was another happy hunting ground for Japanese mercenaries and merchants alike, with a frequent blurring of the distinction between them.

The most famous samurai ever to serve abroad was Yamada Nagamasa, who fought for the King of Siam and was given in return a Siamese princess for his wife and the governorship of a province. The confidence he enjoyed from the king inevitably led to jealousy and accusations of power politics, some of which were well founded, as when the Japanese became involved in the royal succession. The affair ended with an attack on the Japanese settlement and the expulsion of its inhabitants, but

eight samurai had been absent on a pilgrimage to a Buddhist temple, and were arrested on their return and put in jail.

Some foreign pirates, probably Cambodian, came to hear of the departure of the Japanese troops and took the opportunity to raid Siam. The Siamese king, realizing that the Japanese "belonged to a nation more feared by the Southerners than a fierce tiger," promised his captives their liberty if they would help rid his country of the invaders. The Japanese acted with alacrity, and proposed that as many Siamese as possible should be equipped with Japanese armor and helmets (the sight of which would terrify the attackers) and that eight elephants should also be made available. Seventy suits of Japanese armor were found, and the Siamese were dressed up in them. The eight samurai took command of them, as well as an extra 500 Siamese soldiers, and placed a couple

Above: The city of Nagasaki, one of the most important sites in Japan to be associated with early contacts between Japan and the West.

of small cannon on the back of each elephant on its howdah. As soon as they came in sight of the pirate ships, they began their furious cannonade, which would speedily have sunk the whole fleet, had they not instead prudently retreated.

The Decline of the Samurai

The age of mercenaries and open foreign trade ended in 1639 with the "Closed Country Edict." This was one of the most severe acts by the Tokugawa, and was designed largely to hinder all ties between potential rebel *daimyo* and Catholic Europe, whose missionaries had long been regarded as subversive. The closing off of Japan was never as complete as is popularly believed. Trade with China and Korea continued, and there was still a tiny European presence allowed. These lucky merchants were Dutch, whose Protestant sensibilities made them a much lesser risk. But even they had their activities confined to a tiny artificial island in the middle of Nagasaki harbor. Yet from this tiny enclave that was virtually house arrest, a window stayed open to Europe throughout the Tokugawa period. The Closed Country Edict, however, certainly meant the end of Japanese ventures overseas, and the passing of the age of the samurai mercenaries.

It also issued in two centuries of peace, and this provided a further challenge to the samurai class. Paradoxically, it is these outcast samurai whom we have been discussing who were to

Right: A mounted samurai, preceded by a flag bearer and attended by a groom, from a painted scroll in the Shinshiro Museum.

Far right: The Iskikawa Gate, the only remaining section of the castle of Kanazawa, seat of the *daimyo* Maeda Toshiie.

make the greatest contribution to the best-known development associated with the samurai during the Tokugawa period. This was the emergence of the martial arts out of the martial disciplines of the Age of War. There is ample evidence that the mainstream martial skills with bow, spear, and sword suffered something of a decline among the shogun's own warriors and had been replaced by a mixture of arrogance and indifference. The author Ogyu Sorai (1666–1728) denounced what he saw as the bad behavior of the samurai class:

They conduct themselves in the town with their fearful appearance and their thrust-out elbows. With their power to punish they suppress people and create disorder in society...They merely study the stories of warfare and the combative method. Or, perhaps they believe that the mere acquisition of their professional skills is the way of the warrior.

Other writers complained that the samurai seemed to have washed their hands of the

Above: A model of the Dutch settlement at Dejima in Nagasaki Bay, the artificial island that provided Japan with its only contact with Europe following the Seclusion Edict of 1639.

Above: Nowadays the symbol of the cherry blossom as representing the brief lives of samurai is commemorated by annual cherry blossom viewing parties, as in this example at Tenri.

martial arts altogether, and handed over this precious inheritance to the lower classes in society including opportunistic criminals. In 1650, a law was introduced that banned dueling among bored samurai and in 1690, a law was even passed to compel samurai to practice the martial arts! But one must have some sympathy with the samurai of Edo. They were forced to live on a fixed stipend in a world where prices were rising and the townspeople appeared to

be much better off than they were. Many turned to trades or to arts and crafts to supplement their incomes. In 1720 it was noted that in the city of Kanazawa the samurai were spending more time making pots and pans than being warriors. Some, apparently, even pawned their sword blades, replacing them with strips of bamboo when inspections or guard duty happened. Another critic of the samurai character, Murata Seifu (1746–1811) wrote that "only the swords in their belts remind them that they are samurai." It is just as well that Murata did not have much opportunity to examine these swords!

Yet there was little that any writer could do to reverse the overall trend toward decline in a peacetime army, and it is noticeable that when the shogunate was overthrown, the revolutionaries were revealed to have studied and practiced the martial arts in secret. These were the men who were to forge a new and modern Japan, and create a world where all samurai looked like being forgotten except in legend and art, but where their memories now grew stronger as the years went by.

The Meiji Restoration

The great paradox of the Meiji Restoration of 1868, whereby the Tokugawa shogunate was overthrown and replaced by a Japanese government determined to modernize the country, was that the initial impetus for getting rid of the shogun came from men who wanted instead to resist the Western world. They were horrified as they saw the shogun's officials negotiate treaties with foreign powers that would open up Japan's ports. The western clans of the Choshu area were particularly insistent on the expulsion of foreigners. In response to their entreaties, the shogunate informed Choshu that the expulsion would begin on the tenth day of the fifth lunar month of that same year (1863). That the shogun could not only contemplate the impossible, but give one month's notice of its execution, may have

meant that they were playing for time. It also could have indicated that they were encouraging Choshu to precipitate a crisis that would concentrate foreign anger on to that troublesome territory.

The leaders of Choshu, however, took the whole matter at its face value. As there were no foreigners in Choshu to expel, the energies of the Han were directed against the foreign ships that made use of the Shimonoseki strait that skirted its shores. One thousand men were set to work building forts along the coastline. A military specialist in Western learning was invited from Nagasaki to advise the Han, and the seat of government was moved from Hagi, which was vulnerable to sea borne attack, to Yamaguchi.

On the day appointed for the expulsion of the foreigners, Choshu alone out of all Japan carried out the order by firing on a United States merchant ship en route from Shanghai to Yokohama that just happened to be in the wrong place at the wrong time. Two weeks later it attacked a French ship as it passed through the straits. Retribution was swift. Within days another American ship had appeared, and when it was bombarded from the Choshu forts at Hagi and Shimonoseki it replied in kind, damaging the forts and sinking two gunboats that Choshu had only recently purchased. Four days later, a French warship appeared and shelled the Choshu forts. They then put up a landing party, destroyed the forts and their ammunition, confiscated most of the weapons and set fire to local houses. A letter on the incident from the Choshu Han read:

The initial impetus for getting rid of the shogun came from men who wanted instead to resist the western world.

直江山城守兼継

荒川豊後守

Right: Naoe Kanetsugu,
the celebrated *daimyo* of northern
Japan, who opposed the Tokugawa
rise to power.

On the first day of the sixth month, a single United States ship destroyed two gunboats at Hagi. On the fifth day it destroyed all the forts both at Hagi and Chofu and half of the Hagi castle. Seven or eight hundred persons were killed, thus throwing Shimonoseki and Hagi into utter disorder…Everyone was making preparations to flee. I have heard that even peasants and merchants gnashed their teeth murmuring, "Are the samurai such good-for-nothings?"

The attacks did nothing to convince Choshu that their policy was wrong. That came a year later as a consequence of a massive four nation fleet action against them in 1864. For now they saw no more than the need to carry out military reforms on Western lines. The job was given to Takasugi Shinsaku, who was currently under house arrest for having gone up to Kyoto without the *daimyo*'s permission. Takasugi proposed forming a militia of samurai and peasants that would be kept separate from regular army units. It represented a change of heart with regard to samurai status that had been gaining ground in Japan for years. Before the arrival of Commodore Perry, for example, the influential Murata Seifu had written that possession of arms by the peasantry should be resisted as "it would result in the loss of distinction between the upper and lower classes." Even he had changed his tune by 1854, and argued that not only should peasants be trained, but that gunnery practice would do no harm if it was extended to Buddhist priests as well.

In spite of samurai misgivings over the demeaning nature of drilling peasants and a long distaste for firearms, the fear of the foreigner was so great that Takasugi Shinsaku found that he was pushing against an open door. Where Choshu led, so they expected the other Han to follow, and when this response was not forthcoming Choshu's attitude became even more extreme, and a battle took place to secure the imperial palace:

Below: Statue of Sakamoto Ryoma, one of the heroes of the Meiji Restoration.

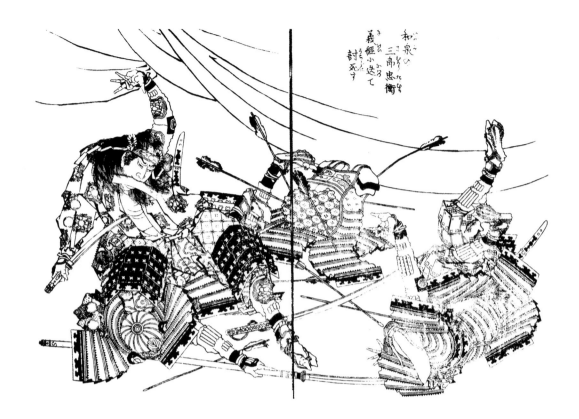

Right: Fighting to the last, the samurai prepares to commit *hara-kiri* in this drawing by Hokusai.

Opposite page: Saigo Takamori, the "last of the samurai," who led the doomed Satsuma Rebellion in 1877.

The two lines were facing each other, poised with rifles and cannon...Squads were formed, the lines were drawn, both sides wore armor, and holding themselves in readiness, each glared at the other. Choshu did not falter in the least...and did not draw back although faced with a desperate situation; it was truly heroic. Among the Choshu forces were youths of 15 or 16 wearing headbands of white silk and carrying western rifles; their eyes betrayed no fear of the huge army confronting them....Choshu, which alone advocated righteousness and loyalty, had set up several tens of cannon, but all pointed downward so as not to point towards the abode of the emperor.

Eventually the Choshu forces withdrew, but the following year they were back, still eager to assert themselves. They arrived in Kyoto in full armor, and when asked by one guard detachment why they were so attired received the reply that the samurai of Choshu always wore battledress in readiness for a barbarian attack. In the event it was the Choshu army that went into the attack, and after a short skirmish were repulsed from the palace as conclusively as they had been in 1863.

Other battles took place during these tumultuous years. In addition to more conventional battles, assassination and ambush played a role in a way unheard of since the days of the *ninja* in the Sengoku period. Brotherhoods of samurai fought on both sides with swords and modern rifles. In one incident, a group of 21 young samurai from Aizu-Wakamatsu kept the flag of the Tokugawa flying as the imperialists advanced. The group, called the *Byakkotai* or "White Tigers," retreated to Mount Iimori, from where they could see Aizu-Wakamatsu's castle apparently going up in flames. Believing that all was lost they resolved to go to their deaths like the samurai of old, and committed *hara-kiri* on the mountainside. In fact, their sacrifice was in vain because the castle had not fallen—but it made the White Tigers into one of the last exponents of the ideal of the way of the warrior.

The wars of the Meiji Restoration succeeded in taking back from the Tokugawa family the commission of shogun that had first been given to Minamoto Yoritomo 800 years earlier. A young and energetic emperor was now on the throne. He was a man who encouraged modernization, and insisted that Japan could learn much from the West. His reforming zeal was not to the liking of many from the old samurai class, whose privileges had been taken from them. One man, Saigo Takamori, led a rebellion in Satsuma province and laid siege to the troops of the new Western-style conscript army in Kumamoto Castle. At one stage Kumamoto witnessed the remarkable sight of sword-wielding samurai clambering up the walls against soldiers armed with the latest European rifles, but it was the forces of modernity that triumphed in the end. The Satsuma Rebellion of 1877 ended with the suicide of Saigo Takamori, the man who was truly the last of the samurai.

CHAPTER 3

samurai organization and daily life

The organization within a successful samurai army would consist of a hierarchy of relationships.

Right: A well-preserved samurai house in the conservation area of Nagamachi in the city of Kanazawa.

Opposite page: A parade of samurai taking part in the "Alternate Attendance" system's requirement of a visit to Edo to pay respects to the shogun.

Right: An old samurai house preserved in a remote corner of the Japanese mountains, far from modern traffic.

Of the "glue," which held the samurai clans together, family ties were the strongest and then the longstanding relationships between lord and vassal. Someone born into a warrior house would be trained from boyhood in the skills and attitudes necessary to become a samurai worthy of his ancestors. The organization within a successful samurai army, therefore, would consist of a hierarchy of vertical relationships—family, vassal, or both—linked horizontally by other ties of marriage, agreed responsibility, or obligation. An example of the latter would be a debt of honor to a warrior who had saved another's life. Among the weakest ties of all were alliances between clans, which were particularly prone to break once battle had been joined, and a halfhearted

alliance quickly became treason. The large-scale battles of the sixteenth century contain several examples of this, but such activities are less common in the smaller wars of the Gempei period.

Comparatively weak social ties existed in the case of the foot soldiers who tilled a samurai's fields but did not possess any family links or aspirations to social status. Yet even these were loyal and valued compared to the peasant warriors, recruited virtually by press gang, who were poorly equipped and so carelessly registered that any desertion was untraceable. The Taira army that pursued Minamoto Yoshinaka in 1183 lost much of its strength from peasant desertion before it even came in sight of the enemy.

The Command Structure in the Heian Period

Throughout Japanese history those who bore the title of samurai were the elite of any army, a status conveyed originally by the possession of these two essential items of equipment: a bow and a horse. Yet there was no time when these elite samurai were not supported by hundreds of foot soldiers and there was always some organization to the system, even if the accounts of samurai warfare of the Heian period do not often give the impression of being carried out by disciplined and drilled armies.

It is true that the collapse of the Chinese-style conscription system in A.D. 702 meant the passing of organized infantry units, but this meant that the discipline and organization in a samurai army of the Heian period was to be found in units smaller than the overall army. The limits of such organization were probably small groupings on the battlefield of 20 or so warriors who supported each other, linked by family or other ties. Their companions would have been relatives or comrades with whom they had trained and had fought previously side by side. Such a group would have been able to coordinate their movements among the overall chaos of a samurai battle. While one of their number fought his worthy opponent, the others provided support. The close cooperation between the Minamoto relatives during the night attack that constituted the Hogen Rebellion is a successful example of this.

The social organization of an army was reflected in its behavior on the battlefield and during the Heian period, samurai warfare consisted of two major types of battlefield activity: *ikkiuchi* (single combat) and group combat. The first type will be described later (see Chapter 7). The second is that of the general fight on the battlefield, into which attendants and lowly peasants would be drawn—though in all the accounts of the period, the impression given is

The social organization of an army was reflected in its behavior on the battlefield.

Left: A procession of a *daimyo* between Kyoto and Edo, typical of the "Alternate Attendance" system introduced by the third Tokugawa shogun Iemitsu.

Above: A servant prepares food while an attendant carries a lacquer tray through to his lord. This diorama is in Kokura Castle, Kyushu.

that it is the fighting of samurai against samurai that constitutes samurai warfare. Within this general fighting may be identified a certain coordination between small groups committed to the overall battle plan, but with a prime loyalty to each other, in an organizational system which did not stifle the demands of individual glory. Samurai organization, therefore, worked with two potentially competing agendas: the individual and the group. The mark of the successful commander during the Heian period was the ability to balance the two to his own, and his followers, mutual advantage.

The Command Structure in the Sengoku Period

Similar patterns of organization and warfare continued until the mid-sixteenth century. For much of samurai history, most armies were disbanded at the end of a campaign and their

members sent back to work in the fields, so that some samurai, and virtually all the *ashigaru* (foot soldiers), would return to their lands to be summoned again when the need arose. But once the *daimyo* began to realize that their troops, and their training and experience, were a precious asset that they could not afford to lose at the end of a campaign, systems of organization were introduced that paralleled the move toward uniformity of equipment and appearance. The organization of a sixteenth-century samurai army therefore took two forms: a hierarchical command structure, invariably headed by samurai and not unlike the time of the Gempei Wars, and the innovation of a considerable degree of specialization in weapons and functions, which was chiefly concerned with the *ashigaru*.

Just as in the Heian period, the samurai hierarchy depended on factors such as birth, hereditary vassalage, examples of loyal service, and so on, and had a considerable social as well as military aspect. At the apex of the pyramid was the individual *daimyo*, and next to him were his own family members and relatives. Next in rank were the hereditary retainers of the family, known as the *fudai,* who had served the lord for many years. Their sons would act as pages to the *daimyo* in peacetime. Their own vassals formed the next tier of service, to be followed by those who had been taken on or absorbed following the defeat of their lords.

The bonds of trust linking the *daimyo* to this group could be very strong, because unlike the popular image of a defeated army committing

一魁随筆勇傳

治部大輔天源義基

一家略傳史
柳下亭
種員記

Left: Imagawa Yoshimoto was one of the most successful *daimyo* of the Sengoku period, until the year 1560 when he attempted to march on Kyoto. All that lay between him and his objective was Oda Nobunaga's tiny army in Owari province. Having overrun Nobunaga's frontier castles, Yoshimoto set up camp and held a head-viewing ceremony. Nobunaga led a surprise attack and Yoshimoto was killed. He is shown in this print sitting on a typical general's folding camp stool, giving directions with his *saihai* (baton of command).

mass suicide after a defeat, joining the enemy was very common. Instead of beheading the defeated, the realists among the *daimyo* began to recycle them. The hoary myth of a samurai's undying and unflinching loyalty to his lord, which had a basis in solid fact, ran into difficulties when that lord was either defeated or dead. Defeated *daimyo* were often encouraged to surrender their territories for the guarantee of

being reinvested in their original holdings in exchange for a pledge of allegiance. A good example is the process by which Takeda Shingen expanded his domains. Rivals such as the Sanada of Shinano were first defeated then absorbed, and their leaders took their places among the Takeda "Twenty-Four Generals," Shingen's most trusted retainers. When the Takeda were defeated in their turn in 1582,

Right: A Japanese war drum mounted on a static frame. Similar but smaller versions were carried into battle on the backs of *ashigaru*.

kami, who held Tawara Castle for the Hojo family at the time of Toyotomi Hideyoshi's expedition against them in 1590. We do not have a detailed analysis of their weaponry, but the army was broken down as follows:

Mounted samurai	75
Foot samurai	36
Ashigaru	115
Laborers	26
Total	**252**

Raising an Army

For most of the Warring States period, and among the majority of the samurai class, the notion of raising an army was a process that the samurai left up to others. The samurai himself, unless he was a part-time farmer, was expected to keep in military readiness, with armor, weapons, and a horse. In addition, he was expected to provide other troops in the lord's service, with the amount and level of equipment depending upon the samurai's recorded wealth, which was expressed in terms of the assessed yield of the rice fields he possessed. Such assets were measured in *koku*, one *koku* being the amount of rice thought necessary to feed one man for one year. This is how the *ashigaru* entered the story. The samurai knew exactly how many men he was required to take with him on campaign. Some would be other samurai, who were more than likely to be related to him in some way. The *ashigaru* would not have the same relationship, but as the years went by and casual recruitment became less

many of their number passed over into the service of the victorious Tokugawa.

The fighting *ashigaru* (foot soldiers) of the Warring States period were divided into the three major weapon functions of arquebus, spear, and bow. There were also *ashigaru* who acted as samurai attendants, standard bearers, drummers, and the like. Many *ashigaru* were employed in carrying flags, as these were a vital tool for battlefield communication and martial display.

Below the *ashigaru* were an amorphous mass of casual baggage carriers and laborers who were press-ganged into service like the peasants of old. Until Hideyoshi's Separation Edict of 1591, such men had the opportunity of becoming fighting men, but with the passing of this important law, the line was to be drawn forever between samurai and farmers. It is also interesting to note that in the *daimyo* armies that fought in Korea half the number of men transported overseas were these common laborers and other non-combatants.

A good example of the command delegated down to an individual samurai is Nagato no

common, a tradition of service to a particular samurai family would develop. A samurai's *ashigaru* followers, therefore, would be drawn from the workers on the samurai's lands, thus completing the final tier of feudal obligation.

When it was necessary for the army to assemble, either for an actual campaign or for review and training purposes, those who would normally live out in the villages, including nearly all the *ashigaru* and some of the lower

Above: Baggage carriers follow their lord in one of the "Alternate Attendance" processions.

Left: A *horagai* or conch shell trumpet, a useful device for signaling in battle.

ranking samurai, would be advised by a runner. He would give as many days notice of the muster as was practically possible. Over the next few days, the *ashigaru* would assemble his armor and weapons and make whatever repairs were necessary to his equipment. He would have been told to listen for the sound of the *horagai* (conch shell trumpet), drum, or bell that would indicate the hour to move off. Early one morning therefore, such a sound would ring out, and the *ashigaru* would meet each other on the road as they made their way to the agreed place of assembly. This might involve a two or three hour walk. Here they would be drilled and inspected by the samurai whose responsibility it was to supply these men for the war effort. Following the roll call, the samurai would lead the contingent in a march to the castle, where they would swell the numbers arriving. Once the entire army was assembled, a decision would be made about who and how many would stay behind to strengthen the garrison, and then the army would set off for war.

Raising an army could proceed at an organized pace providing that the enemy were nowhere near. However, emergency situations, such as an invasion of one's province by an enemy, did not allow the leisurely assembly described above. In such a situation, the farmers needed to become *ashigaru* within hours rather than days, which implied considerable readiness and preparation on their part, and an efficient internal communications system to enable the call to arms to be transmitted rapidly. The Takeda, for example, used an efficient system of fire beacons.

Right: The keep of Himeji Castle, regarded as the finest in Japan, seen at cherry blossom time.

Castles and Mansions

Following Hideyoshi's Separation Edict armies became more and more professional in the sense that they were physically separated from the land, and lived in barracks in the castle towns while the farmers stayed outside in the countryside. In the castle towns, a samurai's rank could be ascertained by looking up where he lived on a map. Just as Edo Castle, the seat of the shogun, was surrounded by the *daimyo*'s *yashiki* (mansions), so the *daimyo*'s own castle towns back in the provinces followed the same pattern. Around their castles, where the family and some senior retainers lived, were the homes of the other retainers, their distance from the castle walls being in roughly direct

Left: The main entrance to the Ise Sengoku Village, made to look like the main gate of a samurai's castle of the mid-sixteenth century.

proportion to their rank. The higher retainers, the *karo,* were placed just outside the keep within the castle walls proper, the samurai were in between, and the *ashigaru* were outside the actual walls, and sometimes protected by a moat or an earthen wall. Between the two groups of samurai and *ashigaru* retainers lay the quarters of the favored merchants and artisans, most of whom would be engaged in trading and producing the goods that were in demand from the samurai class. Outside the ring of *ashigaru's* barracks lay the designated quarter of temples and shrines, whose buildings acted as an outer defense cordon, and from where the roads could be sealed off and guarded. From the edge of the castle town began the fields of the farmers, who grew the rice to support those within the town's boundaries.

The appearance of the samurai barracks was of an almost unbroken street frontage, save where a few large gateways, composed of heavy timbers strengthened with iron clamps, were interposed to relieve the monotony of the general style of architecture. The buildings mostly stood upon low stone foundations, surrounded by small ditches. The windows are barred, and the general aspect was gloomy in the extreme. The inhabitants of the barracks, however, did not spend all that much time there, because the samurai had no wars to fight after 1639, so much of their time was to be spent either marching to Edo or marching away

Right: The garden of the palace of Nijo Castle in Kyoto, is a harmoniously designed to complement the house.

Right: The *yashiki* (mansion) of the Toda *daimyo* in Iga Ueno, a representative example of a large-scale dwelling for a *daimyo* in the early Edo period.

Left: The beautiful castle of Matsumoto, looking across the wet moat toward the tower keep, built in 1597.

Far left: A view of Hiroshima Castle from the early twentieth century.

from it. This was because their *daimyo* was only able to live in his *yashiki* one year out of two, the alternate year being spent back in his castle town. This so-called *sankin kotai* ("Alternate Attendance" system) was the most unusual, and the most successful, of all the means the Tokugawa shoguns were to devise for reducing the risk of rebellion from the *daimyo*. In essence, it was no more than hostage taking on a colossal scale, because the *daimyo*'s wife and children lived always in the *yashiki* in Edo, while the *daimyo* himself alternated his residence between his fief and the capital.

The other aspect of the system was that the muster lists which, in times of war, had regulated a *daimyo*'s feudal obligations in terms of the supply of men and equipment for war, were continued into peacetime. The lists prescribed the size and equipment of the retinue of samurai and *ashigaru* which the *daimyo* would be expected to have accompany him on his alternating trips. As stipends were fixed, and there were no fresh lands to conquer, the cost of the "Alternate Attendance" system kept the *daimyo* in a state of genteel poverty, and probably constant worry, but certain *daimyo* with particular defense responsibilities were allowed a reduced commitment. The So *daimyo* on the island of Tsushima, which lies between Japan and Korea, only had to reside in Edo for four months in every two years.

A similar concession applied to the little known but strategically vital *daimyo* of the Matsumae family on the northernmost island of Hokkaido. The other *daimyo* had to march at the head of a huge army, gorgeously dressed and ready for battle, either to Edo or back again, once every twelve months.

When the procession of the Maeda *daimyo*, the richest in Japan after the Tokugawa, (whose income was a staggering 1,250,000 *koku*), left Kanazawa in the mid-seventeenth century, it consisted of no less than 4,000 samurai, but within a hundred years the financial burden forced a reduction in numbers to 1,500. There is also a pathetic note in the account books of the Inaba *daimyo* referring to additional expenses encountered in 1852 after being overtaken by darkness in the Hakone mountains. The *daimyo* suddenly found himself compelled to purchase 8,863 candles and 350 pine torches, as well as hiring extra porters and lantern bearers.

But if the *sankin kotai* was a burden to the *daimyo*, it proved otherwise to his retainers. There was the prospect of a long, but not unpleasant journey, much of which would be along well-trodden highways. The two main roads linking Edo with Kyoto were the Tokaido, which followed the Pacific sea coast, and the Nakasendo, which wended its way through the mountainous interior. As early as 1604, three decades before the *sankin kotai* was introduced, a system of post stations was introduced along the Tokaido. By 1633, an efficient post horse and courier system was completed that reduced the traveling time for the 300 mile journey from Nihombashi in Edo to Sanjobashi in Kyoto to a mere ten days. By frequent changes of horses, couriers could make the journey in three days. Needless to say a *daimyo*'s procession was conducted at a much more leisurely pace, making good use of the "Fifty-three stations of the Tokaido" immortalized in the prints of Hiroshige.

Bushido

Prior to these peaceful times, of course, the samurai were men of war. Being faced with the horrors of war on a daily basis, and with the likelihood of one's own death ever present, it would be foolish to think of any samurai being blind to the reality of his calling. Exaggerated accounts such as *Heike Monogatari* performed the function of making the practice of war into something acceptable and bearable, and the samurai responded to the realities of their profession with a mixture of group solidarity, nostalgia, and snobbery. In Europe it was called chivalry. In Japan, in the early years of the Edo period it was known as *bushido*. However, the foundations of it were there centuries before in the loyalty and bravery that tradition demanded from the lowliest samurai. The code itself may have been unwritten, but the exploits of one's ancestors provided sufficient case studies for its precepts to be thoroughly understood, even if they could not always be realized.

The classic work on *bushido* is *Hagakure*, compiled by a samurai in the service of the Nabeshima, but it also includes practical advice on samurai behavior such as:

The samurai responded to the realities of their profession with a mixture of group solidarity, nostalgia, and snobbery.

Every morning the samurai of 50 to 60 years ago would bathe, shave their foreheads, put lotion in their hair, cut their fingernails and toenails rubbing them with pumice and then with wood sorrel, and without fail pay attention to their personal appearance. It goes without saying that their armor in general was kept free from rust, that it was dusted, shined, and arranged.

And:

When one departs for the front, he should carry rice in a bag. His underwear should be made from the skin of a badger. This way he will not have lice. In a long campaign, lice are troublesome.

Much of *Hagakure* is concerned with death, and it is very tempting to look back from our modern world and see the cult of *bushido* and its death-defying loyalty as ways of coping with the horrors of war, or even of assuaging guilt by sanitizing its profession on pages of chronicles where civilians never appear. To counter this view, it has to be noted that the samurai appear to have had no guilty feelings whatsoever about what they did, including the massacres in Korea. In Yoshino Jingoza'emon's account of the fall of Pusan in 1592, Japan's first victory of the war, he writes of the orgy of slaughter during which the frenzied samurai even cut the heads off dogs and cats, but it is all reported in a very matter-of-fact way. One is driven to the conclusion that the reality of war

from which the chroniclers attempted to shield their readers was no more than the reality that wars were actually fought between anonymous groups of vulgar soldiers in an obscuring fog of cannon smoke, a concept that may indeed have held real terror for the proud and individual samurai.

The greatest element of unreality that appears in the chronicles is that accounts such as the exploits of Minamoto Yoshitsune in *Heike Monogatari* and Kusunoki Masashige in *Taiheiki* set impossible and largely fictionalized standards of conduct to which later generations might aspire. The result was that although Japanese battles in the Warring States period

Above: A painted scroll depicting a *daimyo* of the early Edo period from the Sakai family.

Right: A samurai is knocked off his horse during the fight on the beach that followed the storming of the fortress of Ichinotani in 1184. The exploits from these earlier wars inspired the samurai of the sixteenth century.

were won through a skilful if unglamorous combination of samurai, foot soldiers, and artillery, it was nostalgia, an appeal to precedent, and the cherished ideals of individual combat that still ruled supreme in the samurai mind. Thus it was that the capture of Ch'ungju, a particularly bloody struggle in Korea, was compared romantically to the battle of Ichinotani in 1184, and the decision of whether to attack at the battle of Chiksan in 1597 took into account the similarity of its situation to Nagashino.

One major difference between European chivalry and *bushido* is the total absence of courtly love from the Japanese version. The European knight, fighting with his lady's sleeve affixed to his helmet and dashing off a quick sonnet when there was a lull in the fighting, has no samurai equivalent. In the *Gikeiki,* the life of

Minamoto Yoshitsune, there is a scene where the hero seduces a young woman, but his underlying motive is the acquisition of a Chinese military scroll possessed by her father! When women appear in the accounts of samurai heroism it is usually in a self-immolating role as they commit suicide when a castle falls, such as the wife of the keeper of Sakasai Castle who lifted the castle's bronze bell on to her shoulders and drowned herself in the moat.

A very important factor in *bushido* was the emphasis placed on a willingness to die for one's lord or for the cause, and the ultimate expression of this was the committing of *seppuku,* otherwise known as *hara-kiri,* the act of ritual suicide, which was admired by friend and foe alike. In Europe, the rare mentions of suicide after a battle are invariably the result of panic and terror, and are never seen as a noble

Left: A woodblock print depicting the Igagoe Vendetta, one of the most celebrated acts of revenge by samurai during the Edo period.

deed. Torii Mototada fought against hopeless odds at Fushimi in 1600 to buy time for his master Tokugawa Ieyasu, and then killed himself in dramatic fashion to avoid the disgrace of capture.

Samurai also committed suicide to make amends for an error, such as the example of Yamamoto Kansuke, who killed himself at the battle of Kawanakajima in 1461 when he perceived that his battle plan had gone disastrously wrong and took responsibility for the failure in this most dramatic fashion. Suicide could also be an act of protest, or a way to follow one's lord in death. An account in *Taikoki* tells of Reizei Motomitsu at Ulsan in 1598, who, "wielded his *naginata* like a water wheel, slaying fifteen or sixteen of the nearby enemy," and was cut down, to the great distress of his followers:

Because [they] were by chance somewhere else, they regretted that they had not been there with him to be killed in battle, so when they took possession of Motomitsu's corpse they performed the act of cutting open their bellies in the shape of a cross on that very spot.

The greatest tenet of *bushido* lay in the area of self-belief, because the mere existence of a warriors' code reinforced the samurai's perception of themselves as an elite. When Kato Kiyomasa attacked the Jurchens of Manchuria in 1592, his sole motivation was "to show the savages the mettle of the Japanese," and in reporting the siege of Namwon, Okochi Hidemoto refers to foot soldiers as "our inferiors." Samurai were always a race apart, and even in the new situation of huge armies of disciplined infantry, the aristocratic sentiment seems to have been that the larger your army, the greater your need to stand out from the crowd. For example, when somber and practical battledress armors became universally adopted in Japanese armies of the late sixteenth century, so their equally robust and sensible helmets became embellished with all sorts of weird and wonderful crests and adornments, from huge wooden buffalo horns to plumes of peacock feathers, all of which are regularly noted as being worn during the heat of battle.

Bushido also included the personal involvement in battle of a country's leaders, or of its would-be leaders. A commander may have been supposed to stay on his camp stool at the rear, protected by his bodyguard, but there were few generals who could resist joining in the fray. Thus the young Tokugawa Ieyasu returned from the battle of Azukizaka in 1564 and stripped off his armor, at which three bullets fell out of his shirt. In 1576, Oda Nobunaga was wounded in the leg while conducting operations against the Ikko sectarians of Ishiyama Honganji, three years after his great rival Takeda Shingen had been mortally wounded by a bullet fired from the besieged castle of Noda. When Toyotomi Hideyoshi failed to cross over to Korea to command his army in person he provided one of the few examples in Japanese history when a leader did not take the lead. Even as late as 1615, the now retired shogun Tokugawa Ieyasu was personally involved in combat at Osaka and was wounded by Sanada Yukimura.

Right: Oda Nobunaga, from a painted hanging scroll in Inuyama.

Far right: The actor Nakamura Shikan in the role of Kawai Matagoro, who sparked the act of revenge known as the Igagoe Vendetta.

Mass Suicide

Following the fall of Kamakura in 1333 there was a mass suicide by the Hojo Regents. When the battle was seen to be lost, they determined to die like true samurai, and *Taiheiki* has preserved the gory record of their departure. Suicide by cutting open the abdomen, the well-known act of *hara-kiri* (belly-cutting) otherwise known as *seppuku*, was a deed of bravery admirable in a samurai who knew he was defeated, disgraced, or mortally wounded. They withdrew from their positions to a temple called the Toshoji, a rather ironic name which means "the temple of the victory in the east." Here, they prepared to commit suicide in the privacy of a cave dug out of the rock at the rear and within the temple.

The Toshoji no longer exists, but the so-called "*hara-kiri* cave" is still there. Although it lies in a remote wooded spot on the fringe of the city center, it still attracts pilgrims. It is rare to visit it and not see fresh flowers as an offering. The one concern among several of the senior *shikken* members was that their leader Hojo Takatoki would not have the courage to commit *hara-kiri* himself. So the others set a precedent. Inside the temple, one samurai "cut his body with a long cut from left to right and fell down, pulling out his intestines…"

In the meanwhile, Nagasaki Shin'uemon, a young boy of 15, bowed before his grandfather, saying, "Assuredly will the Buddhas and gods give sanction to this deed. The filial descendant is he who brings honor to the name of his

Left: Hojo Soun, once a minor samurai who rose to found the dynasty of the Hojo family. He is shown here in the garb of a Buddhist monk.

father." With two thrusts of his dagger he slashed the veins of his aged grandfather's arms. He cut his own belly, pushing his grandfather down and fell on top of him. The young boy's example provided the stimulus that Hojo Takatoki needed. Other samurai cut open their abdomens too, while some, apparently cut off their own heads. In all, 870 samurai and their families committed suicide in the Toshoji.

Thus ended the Hojo Regency, the family that had defeated the Mongols, in a bloodbath almost unparalleled in samurai history. They may have presided over one of the most peaceful centuries in Japanese history, but when they departed out of history they did so in an unprecedented fashion.

Samurai and Civilians

In all ages, war and its horrors have brought death and destruction to those unfortunate enough to be caught up in its wake. Japan, however, was in a somewhat different situation from contemporary Europe. Because nearly all its wars were civil wars, and as the oppressed peasant could easily cross a provincial border to till the fields of an enemy, then surely there was no cruelty against civilians? This is an interesting argument, and in support of this view it must be admitted that the most dramatic example of a peasant uprising against a cruel *daimyo* occurred two decades after the civil wars had ceased. This was the Shimabara Rebellion of 1637–1638, directed against the tyrant Matsukura Shigemasa, who was given to tying peasants inside straw raincoats and setting fire

to them. From this it may be argued that if Matsukura had lived at a time when one's neighbor was by definition one's rival then self-interest alone would have prevented him from acting in such an outrageous manner. It is when the argument is taken one stage further that credulity is strained. The behavior of Japanese forces abroad during the twentieth century is then seen as an aberration of the samurai tradition, and not in any way as its consequence.

It is indeed difficult to tease out much evidence of deliberate civilian casualties from contemporary Japanese writings, though this may simply be that the compilers did not think that such matters were worth recording. When Takeda Shingen was repulsed before Odawara Castle in 1569, he burned the town of Odawara before retiring, but when Toyotomi Hideyoshi

Far left: Toyotomi Hideyoshi and Ishida Mitsunari are shown here together on a statue at Nagahama. Mitsunari first attracted Hideyoshi's attentions because of his skills at the tea ceremony.

Left: Oda Nobunaga, the first of the three unifiers of Japan, as depicted in a waxwork at the Ise Sengoku Village.

took Kagoshima in 1587 and Odawara in 1590 there was nothing that remotely resembled the sack of a European town. By contrast, civilian deaths are implied in the accounts of wars conducted against peasant armies, such as Nobunaga's campaign against the Ikko warrior monks or the Shimabara Rebellion, where the distinction between soldier and non-combatant was blurred and the rebels took shelter in fortresses along with their families.

However, the Korean campaign added a different dimension. Here the fortified town often replaced the isolated castle as a battle site, and many civilian deaths must be inferred from the huge number of heads taken at such conflicts as Chinju and Namwon. But the most powerful evidence comes in the form of a unique and little known document. The *daimyo* Ota

Kazuyoshi took to Korea with him, as personal physician and chaplain, a Buddhist monk called Keinen. Keinen kept a diary in which he recorded his observations and emotions about the human suffering inflicted on the Korean population. Keinen's diary entries covering the fall of Namwon Castle in 1597 make chilling reading. When the castle fell he left the town "and saw dead bodies lying near the road like grains of sand. My emotions were such that I could not even glance at them." As he walked further on he found more bodies in nearby houses, "and this went on into the fields and mountains." The bodies were of innocent men, women, and children. To the samurai chronicler of the Wakizaka family, however, the slaughter was just a further stage of the military operation:

From early dawn of the following morning we gave chase and hunted them in the mountains and scoured the villages for the distance of one day's travel. When cornered, we made a wholesale slaughter of them. During a period of ten days we seized 10,000 of the enemy, but we did not cut off their heads. We cut off their noses, which told us how many heads there were. By this time (Wakizaka) Yasuharu's total of heads was over 2,000.

The collection of noses in lieu of heads was to become a horrid characteristic of the second Korean invasion of 1597–1598.

The collection of noses in lieu of heads was to become a horrid characteristic of the second Korean invasion of 1597–1598. Toyotomi Hideyoshi, who was growing increasingly insane, insisted upon proof of his soldiers' loyalty and achievements, like the reward-giving generals of the ancient civil wars, but the process was hampered by the logistical problems of shipping heads. Hideyoshi therefore began to receive a steady stream of noses, the ghastly trophies being pickled in salt and packed into wooden barrels. Each one was meticulously enumerated and recorded by the *yokome-sh* (inspectors unit) before leaving Korea. In Japan they were suitably interred in a mound near Hideyoshi's Great Buddha, and there they remain to this day inside Kyoto's least-mentioned and most-often-avoided tourist attraction, the grassy burial mound that bears the erroneous name of the Mimizuka, the "Mound of Ears."

In spite of there being several references in the diaries of the Korean Admiral Yi Sun-sin to the practice of sending severed Japanese ears to the Korean Court, the practice from the Korean side was confined to soldiers on the battlefield. Keinen's diary, and several other samurai chronicles, confirm that the Japanese carried out the practice on non-combatants. The chronicle of a certain Motoyama contains the stark and unambiguous statement that "men and women, down to the newborn infants, everyone was wiped out, no one was left alive."

Such observations remind us that the samurai tradition had a very dark side. It may well not have been evident at home, but it was certainly the prevailing image abroad to those who were its victims. Thanks to Keinen, we now know that the samurai may have been no worse than their European counterparts, but they were certainly no better.

The Samurai as Patron of the Arts

It is difficult, when scanning Keinen's diary, to appreciate that the samurai, and especially the *daimyo*, was regarded as the supreme aesthete and the arbiter of good taste. How could the hand that wielded the bloody sword, caress the delicate surface of a tea bowl? This apparent dichotomy between the utterly barbarous and the beautiful is one of the most difficult concepts to understand in the life of the samurai.

It is tempting to discern a certain national trait, an innate ability that comes simply with being Japanese, to translate the most functional of objects into works of art, even to weaponry and instruments of death. That most deadly of

Left: Characters of old Japan depicted in the form of *netsuke* (carved ivory miniatures).

weapons, the Japanese sword, is well recognized as having an outstanding beauty of its own. Somehow the samurai appreciated that perfection of form and perfection of function went hand in hand, and that perfection of form required a commensurate elegance of behavior that complemented the elegance of the surroundings. There is no doubt that the families of *daimyo*, if not all samurai, were trained as extensively in matters of literature and aesthetics as they were in the arts of war. More than one *daimyo* likened the literary and the martial arts as being like the two wheels of a carriage.

The *daimyo* of the latter part of the sixteenth century, of whom Oda Nobunaga and Toyotomi Hideyoshi are the outstanding examples, were considerable patrons of the arts. They employed artists to paint the screens that divided room from room in their palaces, and commissioned potters to produce vessels for the tea ceremony. Their tastes reflected their wealth, enabling them to share in peaceful luxury when not fighting, and it is to Hideyoshi that we owe the elevation of the tea ceremony to an art form. The tea ceremony consists of an aesthetic exercise performed around the simple pleasure of sharing tea with friends. It is at once ritualistic and artistic. It

志賀山の城陥つれ
鬮ぐ々松永久秀
平蛛の茶釜を打砕く

Above: Matsunaga Hisahide smashes a priceless tea kettle to prevent it falling into enemy hands when Shikizan Castle falls to Oda Nobunaga.

Above right: A puppet from the *bunraku* theater in the role of a samurai. *Bunraku* was one of the most popular forms of entertainment during the Edo period.

involves the aesthetic appreciation of the tea bowl from which the tea is drunk, the flower arrangement and the vase which complement it, and the overall design of the tea house and the garden. A rare tea bowl could be more welcome to a *daimyo* than a fine sword, and was frequently much more difficult to acquire.

The great irony of the tea ceremony was that its most prized vessels came from Korea, the country that Japan devastated, so Japanese enthusiasm for the tea ceremony ensured that at least one aspect of Korean culture was respected when the country was invaded. It would certainly have astounded some anonymous Korean potter to hear that a simple peasant's rice bowl he had once made was doing service as a treasured and priceless tea vessel, handled by the greatest in the land. Even before the war Hideyoshi had hired two

brothers, sons of a Korean-born potter, to make the tiles for the roof of his palace of Jrakutei, and under the guidance of the famous tea master Sen Rikyu these ceramic craftsmen had developed the unpretentious but highly prized *raku* style of tea bowl.

When the conquerors prepared to return home in 1598, the opportunity to enrich their own pottery tradition at so little cost was too good to miss. The Shimazu brought 70 Koreans with them to Satsuma, including several potters who began ceramic production in three areas, and two centuries later visitors to Satsuma noted the distinctive Korean dress and language of the communities. It is no coincidence that the *daimyo* who established Korean-operated kilns in their provinces were all passionate devotees of the tea ceremony. Kuroda Nagamasa set up a successful kiln at Takatori

Left: The Noh theater is one of Japan's most precious cultural assets. Noh plays were popular with the samurai. The themes were often taken from samurai history and retold tales of heroism of the ancestors of the ruling classes.

using potters brought from Kyongsang province. Hosokawa Tadaoki put his captives to work at Agano, while the famous name of Arita porcelain is associated with Imari, a town within the fief of Nabeshima Naoshige. Here, in 1616, a Korean potter called Yi Sam-pyong discovered deposits of kaolin-rich clay that led to the first production of porcelain in Japan.

Oda Nobunaga was also a patron of the Noh theater, and is recorded as having chanted some choruses from the Noh play *Atsumori* before setting off to the battle of Okehazama. Noh, like tea and the contemplation of a cleverly designed garden, brought serenity in much the same way as did the practices of the meditative Zen sect of Buddhism, to which many samurai were attracted because of its inner tranquility. But the appreciation of taste gave the cultivated warrior more than a serene and composed mind, however useful that may have proved on the battlefield or in conference. It was also the means that sorted the accomplished man from the common, that proclaimed a subtle ostentation that may sometimes have teetered on the edge of vulgarity, but never quite managed to slip off. This cultivation, this refinement, was the mark of true aristocracy, and was part and parcel of being a *daimyo*, of being an elite among the elite.

Samurai Food and Drink

Any attempt at reconstructing the cuisine of the samurai of medieval Japan must begin with rice, the basic ingredient of Japanese cooking. Rice is a foodstuff that is more than a staple diet. It is almost a sacred object. In Ancient Japan, when the religion we now call Shinto

Above: The preparation of food in camp during the eleventh century. On the left an attendant is carving a raw fish to make *sashimi*. On the right another fellow is jointing what is probably a wild duck.

Above right: The hero Minamoto Yoshiie takes a well-earned meal break during one of his campaigns. His attendant is serving sake (rice wine) in a wooden cup.

was first developing, the worship of numerous *kami* (deities) was carried out by offering them rice and sake, the wine made from fermented rice. The *kami* of food and fertility was second only to Amaterasu the Sun Goddess in adoration, and Inari, the *kami* of rice, was also held in very high esteem. Even in modern Japan the ancient respect for the sacredness of food in general and rice in particular still prevails, and the poetic Shinto prayer for the harvest thanks the *kami* for:

> ...crops in ears long and ears abundant, things growing in the great moor plain, sweet herbs and bitter herbs, things that dwell in the blue sea-plain, the broad of fin and the narrow of fin, seaweed from the offing, seaweed from the shore...

The earliest Japanese diet was therefore sparse and simple, although it was also highly nutritious. It consisted mainly of rice, fish, vegetables, seaweed, salt, and fruit, and was occasionally augmented by the produce of hunting such as venison, wild boar, or game birds.

Japanese cuisine has been influenced over many centuries by its contact with neighboring countries. Early contact with China led to important additions in the form of the soya bean and tea. Soya beans, soy sauce, tofu (bean curd), and miso (fermented soy bean paste) are now among the staples of Japanese cooking. Tea provided for Japan the service that beer provided for northern Europe—it made the water fit to drink.

When the first Europeans arrived in Japan in 1543, the vast difference between the two traditions in matters of food and drink attracted considerable comment. One Japanese *daimyo* (feudal lord) expressed himself baffled by Europeans because, "they eat with their fingers instead of the chopsticks that we use." This lack of understanding was mutual, although a Jesuit missionary acknowledged that the Japanese "live wonderfully healthy lives and there are many old people."

The culinary legacy left behind by the Portuguese included *tempura*. The name apparently derives from the missionaries' practice of fasting, and means the "times" (*tempora*) when they refrained from meat. On these days the Japanese cooks would prepare deep-fried prawns and vegetables in a light batter. This is now one of Japan's most popular dishes.

The courtiers of the Heian period (794–1192), the age which saw the rise of the samurai, lived lives that were elegant and refined but not gastronomically opulent, and the food items noted above would have been seen on their tables as they had been for their ancestors. What was added was a delicacy and artistry in the serving of food, a remarkable tradition that has persisted to this day. Any samurai of the Heian period who enjoyed the company of courtiers would have been fully immersed in this rich tradition of refined and elegant cuisine. The Taira family provides an excellent example in the form of Taira Kiyomori, a warrior who moved in the highest circles of society. Culinary elegance extended to table manners, and a nobleman was expected to leave his bowls perfectly clean, to the extent of tucking pips and fish bones into the sleeves of his robes!

From the fifteenth century onward, similar elegance and refinement became widely practiced among the samurai class through the tea ceremony. By the performance of this highly ritualized way of enjoying a cup of tea in the most refined manner possible, the otherwise bloodthirsty samurai could achieve a mental distraction usually associated only with Zen Buddhism. Zen was in fact an enormous influence on the tea ceremony, which also spawned an entirely new branch of Japanese cuisine:

kaiseki ryori or "tea ceremony cooking," where the contents and arrangement of the dishes are highly symbolic.

Coexistent with the elegant lives of the refined warrior courtiers were the more numerous samurai who lived far simpler lives and ate the same food as the farmers. At the time of the Gempei Wars, such men were often farmers as

Left: A *daimyo* from the Hojo family sits in state and receives food and drink as he consults his senior retainers.

Below: Toyotomi Hideyoshi relaxes at home. A servant girl is in attendance behind him. He is eating a fish using chopsticks.

Above: A samurai feast after a successful battle. The sake (rice wine) is flowing freely.

Fish was preserved by drying or smoking. River fish and game were also available, and samurai were enthusiastic hunters. Particular delicacies included bear's paws, badger's paws, and the crackling from the skin of a roasted wild boar. Meat was preserved by cutting it up and then salting and drying it.

It was only around the middle of the fourteenth century that rice started to become a regular part of a samurai's diet. By the fifteenth century we begin to see a *daimyo*'s wealth expressed in *koku*, one *koku* being the amount of rice needed for one man for one year, and formulae existed so that a *daimyo*'s obligation to supply troops could be calculated from his wealth in *koku*.

A samurai's rice could be cooked in various ways. It might be boiled in a pan, mixed with vegetables or seaweed, steamed or made into *o-nigiri* (rice balls). *Mochi* (rice cakes) were made from rice flour or a mixture of rice and wheat flour. But although rice became far more common as a dish for samurai, the farmers who produced the rice ate very little of it and had to be content with millet, a situation that is reproduced with great feeling in a scene in *Seven Samurai*.

The *Gosannen Kassen Ekotoba* (picture scroll of the Later Three Years' War) is a valuable source of information for samurai cuisine on a campaign fought during the Heian period in the eleventh century. In one section the hero, Minamoto Yoshiie, is shown resting in camp, where he is being served a meal. Yoshiie is shown drinking sake out of a shallow dish, poured out for him by an attendant who uses a

well as warriors, and the Spartan tradition of frugality lived on when these men acquired positions of power. The chronicle *Azuma Kagami* tells us how Minamoto Yoritomo, who became Japan's first shogun, gave a New Year banquet for a high-ranking samurai from the Chiba family where there was only one course: a bowl of rice piled up high with some sake to drink. Ashikaga Yoshiuji, welcoming a visitor, could only offer him dried *abalone* (a shellfish), *mochi* (rice cakes), and sake.

Even when the shogunate was well established, it was still unusual to see samurai eating polished rice except on feast days. They lived mainly on wheat, millet, or a mixture of *gemmai* (husked rice) and wheat. Husked rice was eaten boiled or made into soup, but even poor people were able to augment this fare with *gobo* (burdock), egg plants, cucumbers, mushrooms, and other vegetables. If they lived by the sea there was the addition of fish, shellfish, and seaweed.

large wooden bowl on a long handle. The details in the scroll concerning food preparation are very interesting. In one vignette a samurai is jointing what appears to be a wild duck or a wild goose. Next to him another samurai is shown using a very sharp knife to slice up a fish to produce *sashimi* (raw fish) in exactly the same way as it is prepared today. All he has left is the head, and in another section more *sashimi* is being prepared on a heavy chopping board. One samurai is already using his chopsticks to taste the offerings.

The most poignant use of food by the samurai was through the warrior partaking in a farewell meal prior to setting off on campaign. The dishes consisted of *kachi-guri* (dried chestnuts) probably included because the name can be read as "victory chestnuts," *awabi abalone* (shellfish), *kombu* (kelp), and sake, served in three cups representing heaven, earth, and man. The seafaring pirate families of the Inland Sea had a different tradition of eating octopus before they went to war, as the octopus can defend itself in eight directions at once.

Once the eating of rice became common among the samurai, a warrior would receive his pay in the form of a rice ration. The main problem was how to cook it on campaign, and there exists a famous recommendation from Tokugawa Ieyasu that foot soldiers should be issued with iron helmets so that they could cook rice in them! Alternatively, uncooked rice could be steamed underneath a campfire. The dry rice was placed inside a wet cloth and buried under the fire, where it would cook to perfection. If this could not be done the rice

was baked in a bamboo tube or in emergencies simply steeped in water.

Dried bonito flakes were very nutritious and were light enough to carry easily on campaign. They could make a bowl of rice into a meal. Dried squid and salted fish, dried vegetables, salt, and miso would also find their way into the pan (or helmet). *Umeboshi* (pickled plums) and chilies were two other useful items to eke out a samurai's meal while on campaign. Rice also provided the basis for a very handy convenience food for samurai. Balls of rice called *o-nigiri* were rolled by hand from cooked rice. They could be taken on campaign wrapped in leaves. The rice balls had protein-rich *miso* paste inside, and were reheated by being grilled over a fire.

Above: In this section from the *Gosannen Kassen Ekotoba* (picture scroll of the Later Three Years' War) we see the hero Minamoto Yoshiie resting in between attacks. He is wearing a typical *o-yoroi* armor of the Heian period with a patterned leather breastplate over a *yoroi-hitatare* (armor robe) ornamented with pompoms. On his head is an *eboshi* (cap) and his quiver is at his side. In his hand he holds his signaling fan.

CHAPTER 4

samurai armor and costume

By the twelfth century, most samurai were wearing yoroi *armor of a characteristic box-like design.*

Right: An excavated *tanko-do* (short shell armor), on display in the Gifu Historical Museum.

Opposite page: The *daimyo* Mori Nagayasu, shown in the ceremonial *nagabakama* (long trousers) so designed to make it virtually impossible for the wearer to attempt an assassination.

Right: The details of the simplest type of armor for samurai are shown in this scene from the annual reenactment of Takeda Shingen's departure for war at Kofu.

Below: A warrior dressed in the style of A.D. 500–700. He is wearing the *tanko* style of armor, whereby small metal plates are combined together to make a solid and rigid plate armor, unlike later forms where a flexible corselet was created.

Early Japanese Armor

The earliest armors excavated from Japanese burial mounds were called *tanko*, and are associated with the Yamato state. They were made of heavy iron, the plates being fastened together with leather thongs, and were clearly designed for fighting on foot. Almost all the surviving examples fitted closely to the body and had a pronounced waist so that they sat firmly on the hips.

They were provided with an opening down the front which was fastened by ties of cloth. It must have been difficult to put on, as the strips of iron from which it was made were continuous around the body so that the whole suit had to be sprung open to admit the wearer. This defect was rectified in later models which had a hinged section on the right front or,

occasionally, on both sides. The deep cut-outs for the arms left an extension at the front reaching to the upper chest, and a similar, rather higher section at the back, to which were fastened a pair of cloth shoulder straps which transferred some of the not inconsiderable weight from the hips to the shoulders.

Protecting the lower body and tying over the flanged lower edge of the body armor was a flared skirt, called rather appropriately the *kusazuri* (grass rubber), since it reached to just above the knee. Like the neck guard, it was made of ten or more horizontal pieces, laced to internal leather thongs and split down either side to allow some movement when walking. No protection was provided for the lower legs at this date, but rock carvings show that long baggy trousers were worn, tied with a drawstring just below the knee.

The shoulders and upper arms were covered by an arrangement of curved plates, running from front to back and extending as far as the elbow. Completing the outfit were long, tubular, tapering cuffs of plate fitted with a small panel of leather-laced scales which formed a defensive cover for the back of the hand. As was normal on all later styles of armor, the metal surface was given a coating of natural lacquer as a protection against the humidity of the Japanese climate. Some slight decoration was afforded by leather thongs sewn through holes along the sharp edges of all the major elements, and by a bunch of pheasant-tail feathers tied to iron prongs provided for that purpose on top of the helmet, which had a pronounced beaked front. Fastened through holes in the sides and back of the helmet were a series of broad leather thongs on to which were laced about five horizontal U-shaped strips of iron forming a defense for the neck. Each strip was hung in such a way that it overlapped the one above to leave no gaps, and yet allowed either side or the back to move independently upward with the wearer's movements.

The First Lamellar Armor

Armor made by combining numerous small scales of metal or leather is called lamellar armor. It is of great antiquity having originated somewhere in the Middle East. It was used by the Egyptians and later the Romans, spreading eastward into Central Asia and northward into Eastern Europe, reaching as far as Scandinavia. Although differing in minor details, lamellar

armor was always constructed from more-or-less rectangular overlapping scales or metal or leather laced together into rows which were then laced vertically, each row overlapping the one above so that the tops of the scale heads were visible. The result was a flexible defense whose efficiency lay in its ability to absorb the energy of a blow in the lacing sandwiched between the rows of scales before penetration could begin.

Although the *tanko* continued to be made, the new style of construction was developed into a complementary armor for mounted use called *keiko*. These armors were similar to the armor made and worn in Tibet as late as the nineteenth century. The body of a *keiko* resembled a sleeveless coat opening down the front and with a flared skirt extending to mid-thigh. At the waist was a row of elongated incurved scales that rested on the hips, with sometimes a

Above: Two helmets for samurai, the one on the left having a ridged bowl and a crest, the one on the right has rounded iron rivets holding the separate plates together.

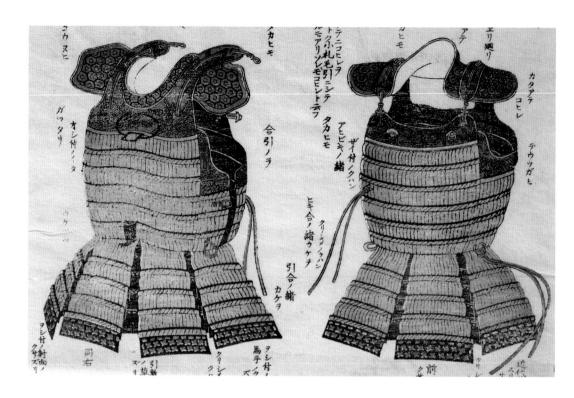

Right: An armor of *do-maru* style.

similar row along the lower edge of the skirt, whose purpose is obscure. Over this was worn a collar and upper-arm guards combination comparable with that worn with the *tanko,* but made entirely of scales. The tubular defense for the forearms was no longer of plates but of narrow vertical splints, this time without any protection for the hand. The legs are always a vulnerable target of a horseman, so leg armor was provided in the form of sections or scales, a tapered section tied above and below the knee and another wrapped around the lower leg with ties at the back.

With the *keiko* came a new style of helmet with a very prominent pierced horizontal peak riveted to the front lower edge. It was lobed in outline and fretted with either a geometric design or one of stylized tendrils. Otherwise it was similar to the *tanko*'s helmet, but had a

circular cup enclosing the top. It has been suggested that this was to accommodate the wearer's hair, but as it was solid it is more likely that the whole arrangement was to carry a plume that would have been tied to the holes in the rim of the upper cup. The neck guard fitted to these helmets was made of metal strips arranged exactly like the earlier ones.

Apart from excavated specimens, another source for what these armor styles looked like are the *haniwa,* the clay figures found in tombs. A large proportion of these represent warriors, and from them it is possible to see the way the two styles of armor evolved and combined, as all possible types of plate and scales were tried out. Some of these helmets and armors are almost identical to those worn in contemporary China and Korea, confirming the close military links between the three countries at this time.

Left: A suit of armor of *haramaki* style (opening at the back) set off with a splendid helmet and a very large *nodowa* (throat guard).

Far left: In this fine hanging scroll Kusunoki Masashige is shown wearing a lavishly decorated *o-yoroi* armor. A white *hachimaki* (headband) is tied round the outside of his *eboshi* (cap). He wears the typical heavy *suneate* (shin guards) and fur boots.

The *Yoroi*

The classic samurai armor called the *yoroi* was no more than a development of the *keiko* style. The *keiko* style continued in use as the foot soldiers' armor, the simple *do-maru,* of which a variant opening at the back rather than at the sides was called a *haramaki.*

By the twelfth century, most samurai were wearing this *yoroi* armor of a characteristic box-like design. As before, it was made from small scales tied together and lacquered, then combined into armor plates by binding them together with silk or leather cords. Each lamella was of iron or leather. A suit made entirely from iron was far too heavy to wear, so the iron scales were concentrated on the areas that needed most protection, and otherwise alternated with leather. The separate parts formed the

yoroi, the classic samurai armor of the Gempei Wars, which provided good protection for the body for a weight of about 30 kilograms.

The main disadvantage of the *yoroi* was not its weight but its rigid and inflexible box-like structure, which restricted the samurai's movement when he was dismounted or using hand weapons from the saddle. If the samurai stayed as a "gun platform" then the *yoroi,* or its more elaborate version the *o-yoroi* was ideal. The body of the armor, the *do,* consisted of four sections. Two large shoulder plates, the *sode,* were worn, which were fastened at the rear of the armor by a large ornamental bow called the *agemaki.* The *agemaki* allowed the arms free movement while keeping the body always covered. Two guards were attached to the shoulder straps to prevent the tying cords being cut, and a sheet of ornamented leather was fastened across the front like a breastplate to stop the bow string from catching on any projection.

The *kabuto* (helmet) bowl was commonly of 812 plates, fastened together with large projecting conical rivets. A peak, the *mabisashi,* was riveted on to the front and covered with patterned leather. The neck was protected with a heavy five-piece neck guard called a *shikoro,* which hung from the bowl. The top four plates were folded back at the front to form the *fuki-gayeshi,* which stopped downward cuts aimed at the horizontal lacing of the *shikoro.* Normally the *eboshi* (cap) was worn under the helmet, but if the samurai's hair was very long the *motodori* (pigtail) was allowed to pass through the *tehen,* the hole in the center of the helmet's crown where the plates met. Some illustrations show samurai wearing a primitive face mask called a *happuri,* which covered the brow and cheeks only. No armor was worn on the right arm, to leave the arm free for drawing the bow, but a simple bag-like sleeve with sewn on plates was worn on the left.

Sengoku Period Armor

The body armor or *do,* was the basis of the whole defensive costume, and as the centuries went by there was a trend to replace the *yoroi* by the simpler *do-maru* of later years. The samurai's *do-maru* had its origin in the simpler suits of armor worn by the foot soldiers who supported the samurai. It was more rounded to the body, with smaller shoulder guards, and

Right: A samurai armed in the fashion of about 1570, in the Ise Sengoku Village.

Far right: A suit of armor typical of the rugged and practical styles of battledress produced during the Sengoku period.

was more suited to fighting on foot or to handling pole arms. One factor determining the appearance of armor was the amount of suspensory lacing. *Kebiki odoshi* (close spaced lacing) was a common style, but this faded in popularity in favor of *sugake odoshi,* whereby the suspensory cords were spaced in pairs. An even simpler version used for breastplates was the *hishiniu* style, whereby the plates were secured using cross knots.

One unusual style was covered in brown leather, which hid the lacing entirely, and is mentioned in an incident during the Japanese invasions when two messengers were dispatched from one Japanese unit to another. The men were wearing leather-covered armor, and were surprised to find themselves staring into 500 gun barrels when they rode up on their errand, because the friendly commander had mistaken them for Korean horsemen!

Sixteenth-century armor was referred to as *tosei gusoku* (modern armor). It was characterized by the addition of armor for the face, thigh guards, and the use of the *sashimono* (flag or other device) on the back. Some suits of armor were sold that proudly displayed dents as they had been tested by having bullets fired at them!

Samurai Clothing

Underneath the armor or other clothes, samurai underwear consisted of a *fundoshi* (loincloth) of white linen or white cotton. In winter it was lined with similar material, but in other seasons it was always single. Both ends (or front and back) were hemmed to put cords through. One of the cords formed a loop to suspend the front end from the neck, and the other secured the back end by being tied in front. The length of the *fundoshi* was about 1.5 meters.

The outer clothes a samurai would expect to wear when not in armor changed very little throughout history. The samurai of the Gempei Wars were men whose proficiency in riding horses was almost a badge of rank, and this is shown in the court costumes of the time, where the clothes have gathered trousers which would be suitable for wearing in the saddle. The armor would be worn on top, but high-ranking warriors would have a *yoroi-hitatare* (armor robe).

The basic male dress during the Sengoku period was the *kimono,* a long, wide-sleeved garment like a dressing gown, reaching to well below the knee. It was sometimes worn over a similarly-shaped undergarment that showed at the neck. It would be held in at the waist by a long sash-like belt which was wrapped two or three times round the body before being tied at the front. Into this belt the samurai would thrust his *katana* and *wakizashi.* The kimono would suffice if the samurai was off to enjoy himself on a summer's evening. Otherwise he would wear in addition a pair of *hakama,* the characteristic samurai trousers. The *hakama* were rather like a divided skirt. They were stiffened and had a low crotch with large openings at the side, and were held in place by two sets of ties at the front and rear, which fastened around the waist. The *hakama* came to the ankle, and when wearing them the swords would still be carried in the belt below.

Below: A suit of armor preserved in a retainer's house in the village of Yagyu.

Right: A samurai in full armor, from a print by Kuniyoshi.

Far right: Yamanouchi Kazutoyo was one of Tokugawa Ieyasu's generals and became a *daimyo* in his own right. Here he is depicted as a sumo wrestler, with the wrestler's *fundoshi* (loincloth) and the hairstyle known as *chasen gami*, where the pigtail stands out.

As indicated in many Japanese movies, the samurai had to be ready to fight at a moment's notice, and when danger threatened he would speedily prepare his loose clothing for the fray. The *hakama* would be hitched up inside the belt, thus allowing the legs free movement, while the sleeves would be tied back with the *tasuki*, a narrow sash that was passed in front of the arms and crossed on the back. An experienced swordsman could perform both tasks in a few seconds.

Unlike the earlier costume, the *hakama* were not suitable for wearing under armor, so he would wear a shirt called a *shitagi*, which was like an ordinary kimono with very narrow sleeves, a little shorter in length and narrower in width, with a few buttons at the breast and a thick tape or cord around the waist. He would also wear *kobakama* (short trousers).

There were a few different styles, generally a little narrower than ordinary *hakama*, and of such a length as will reach about four or five *shaku* below the knees. Everything was held together with an *obi* (under belt) of white linen

or white cotton, folded into four folds. The length depended upon the size of the wearer. It was tied in front, because if it was tied at the back it was then inconvenient to retie if it became loose.

Costume on the Battlefield

On his feet the samurai would wear the type of socks known as *tabi*, which had a separate compartment for the big toe. The *tabi* might be omitted in summer, but the samurai would never go barefoot out of doors. He would usually wear straw sandals called *waraji* or *zori,* or sometimes a pair of *geta,* the high wooden clogs made like a platform. *Geta* would never be worn if there was a chance of danger, because quick movement in them was very difficult. *Waraji* were made from various materials such as hemp, palm fibers, cotton thread, rice straw, etc. There were also various ways of arranging the cords which tie the *waraji* to the feet. It was very important to use an extra tie across the instep when marching on steep,

Left: During the fourth battle of Kawanakajima in 1561, *ashigaru* bring water to their wounded comrades using their helmets as buckets.

snowy, or muddy roads, and in crossing swamps or river sand an extra pair of sandals was just as important as carrying provisions. *Kiahan* (gaiters) were tied on top of the trousers.

Suneate (shin guards) were the first item of armor to be put on. One type, very popular in the Sengoku period, consisted of vertical plates connected by either hinges or chain mail and often, though not always, lined with textile material. There was always a leather guard attached to the inner side of the place that came into contact with the stirrup when riding. *Haidate* (thigh guards) were not formerly worn with *yoroi* but became important in the Sengoku period when the *kusazuri* (tassets) attached to the *do* were reduced in size. It usually consisted of an apron-like piece of cloth a lower part covered with small overlapping

plates of metal or leather. Some also had in addition to the cord at the top edge, cords to tie the lower edge closely against the leg.

Yugake (gloves) were made of tanned skin, and protected the hands, while the *kote* (sleeves) protected the arms. *Kote* were usually of textile material, often silk brocade, padded, laced with small cords upon the inside of the arm, and covered with mail, small metal plates, or quilting having small plates of metal or hide sewn inside each quilt. Covers of metal plates for the back of the hand, were attached to the *kote*. There was the *aigote* version in which the two sleeves are connected.

The *do* (body armor) was the most important piece of armor. Variation from one type to another was largely concerned with the design of the *do*. Two common styles to be found were the *nuinobe do* and the *mogami do*. The

The do *(body armor) was the most important piece of armor.*

Right: A *nodowa*, a guard for protecting the throat.

Far right: A *hoate*, a mask for the face, with added whiskers.

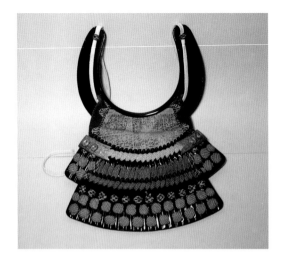

nuinobe do was of two-piece construction, hinged at the left, and the horizontal plates usually had their upper edges finished in a series of semicircles. The *mogami do* was of five-piece construction, and hinged in four places. The horizontal plates of the *mogami do* were usually flanged on their upper edges. Both these styles were commonly laced with *sugake odoshi*, but there existed a "mongrel" style called a *dangaie do* (changed rows do), where the *do* was laced half in *kebiki odoshi* and half in *sugake odoshi*.

The simplest *do* of all was the *okegawa do* which consisted of a solid breastplate and back plate with no lacing. On occasions these plates were made from separate sections riveted together and lacquered over. Some were made to be bulletproof, but the vast majority were just simple suits of armor for *ashigaru*. The more elaborate versions for samurai fell into several categories. The *yokohagi do* had its constituent plates riveted together horizontally, while the *tatehagi do* was fastened vertically. The finest variety of *tatehagi do* were produced by

Myochin Hisaie (1573–1615) who lived in Yukinoshita, from which the style took its name. The *yukinoshita do* had a smooth surface designed to deflect arquebus balls, arrowheads, and sword blades. The *daimyo* Date Masamune outfitted his entire army in *yukinoshita do* armors.

A completely smooth surfaced *do* was referred to as a *hotoke do* (Buddha armor). This smooth surface allowed an artistic armor maker the opportunity to express his art in certain curious ways. One strange creation was the *nio do*, which was hammered to give the appearance of the human torso of an elderly Buddhist monk, with sagging breasts and a bulging stomach. This would often be accompanied by a helmet that was covered in hair dressed like a samurai's coiffure.

An alternative form of decorative armor was *uchidashi do*, which was embossed. This had to be done with care or it would weaken the metal, a fact brought home by an extant specimen dating from 1681 which included the inscription:

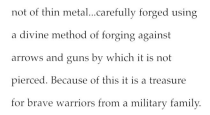

Left: Hojo Soun leads the invasion of Izu province. His foot soldiers unload supplies from a boat. Soun is wearing a Buddhist monk's cowl instead of a helmet.

Far left: Wada Yoshinori is wearing an elaborate pair of *kuwagata* (antlers) on his helmet.

not of thin metal...carefully forged using a divine method of forging against arrows and guns by which it is not pierced. Because of this it is a treasure for brave warriors from a military family.

Increased contact with Europe during the second half of the sixteenth century led to parts from suits of European armor being seen on Japanese battlefields. One example was the *hatomunedo,* or pigeon-breasted cuirass, which had a pronounced central medial ridge.

The *uwaobi* (outer belt) held everything together. *Sode* (shoulder plates) were fastened to the suspenders of the *do* by means of hooks. *Kosode* replaced the larger *o sode* of earlier times. The sword and dagger hung from the belt.

Moving to the head, the *nodowa* protected the throat. The *hachimaki* (head cloth) was put around the head so as to make a padding to receive the helmet. A samurai would comb his hair back and put the center of the cloth behind his head, then wind it round the head and tuck

the ends between the folds. The *hoate* (mask) varied greatly at different periods. The twelfth-century *happuri* covered the temples and the forehead leaving the rest exposed. Later a complete mask was used and still later the half mask, stopping below the eyes and either with or without a nose piece, was evolved. The mask with a nosepiece was called a *mempo.* Whiskers and moustaches could be included. Before putting on the mask a handkerchief was placed between the mask and chin.

There were hundreds of different styles of *kabuto* (helmets) and several different styles of *shikoro,* the neck guard hanging from the back and sides of the helmet. As later styles of armor were very somber, a tradition developed of setting off a fairly plain suit of armor with an elaborate helmet. The "court cap" of Kato Kiyomasa, and the golden "catfish tail" of Maeda Toshiie are well-known examples. Other helmets sported huge wooden buffalo horns or antlers. The use of colored lacquers such as red, gold, or russet brown also made an armor stand out in combat.

The *sashimono* (little banner) was the samurai's heraldic device. The back of the *do* carried at the waistline a socket, and at the level of the shoulder blades a small hinged bridge piece, with a ring on it. These were to support the *sashimono*. There were hundreds of different kinds of *sashimono*, often but not always flags (three-dimensional objects were also used). Flag *sashimono* were usually vertical oblongs, three *shaku* by one *shaku*. The shaft was passed through the ring on the upper part of the back plate of the *do*, its lower end put into the socket behind the waist, and a cord attached to the staff was tied around the body.

The *jinbaori* (surcoat worn over armor) completed the costume for a high-ranking samurai. It was rarely used for fighting, being only a ceremonial garment for use in camp to give a more important appearance to the wearer. It was worn when beginning a march, retreating, at inspections, when triumphantly returning, or when calling upon anyone of higher rank. The curious *horo* (arrow entangler) was a large cloak worn on the back over a basket-work frame. When a samurai was killed in battle, the enemy realized that the dead man was not a common person because of the *horo*, and so the corpse was treated well.

Several medicines and remedies for wounds and sudden illness were carried in a small packet or box. Authorities also recommended the samurai to have a water bottle and some *umeboshi* (pickled plums), together with powder to keep off all sorts of insects.

Early versions of simple plate armor involved having small plates sewn on to a cloth backing and joined by chain mail. This was called *tatami gusoku*, literally "straw mat armor," because it could be folded away. An alternative form that was to become almost universal for the *ashigaru* (foot soldiers) was the *okegawa-do*, which consisted of a solid breastplate and back plate hinged together from which a circle of *kusazuri* (tassets) hung down to the knees. Similar but more elaborate solid plate armors for the samurai, which had the advantage of being bulletproof, provided a similarly inviting surface on which the decorative armorer could display his skills. It was usual for an *ashigaru*'s armor to bear prominently his master's *mon* (badge).

Good armor was vital, and in *Hagakure* we come across the following laconic statement:

> A helmet is usually thought to be very heavy, but when one is attacking a castle or something similar, and arrows, bullets, large rocks, great pieces of wood, and the like are coming down, it will not seem the least bit so.

The Red Regiment

The samurai of the Ii family, the "Red Devils" wore bright red armor. The Taira clan, who were defeated during the Gempei Wars of 1180–1185 fought under red banners, and after their cataclysmic defeat at the battle of Dan no Ura in 1185, the sea is said to have turned red from the dye of the flags and the blood of the slain. But no Taira warrior wore red armor as a mark of clan allegiance, and red lacing seems to

When a samurai was killed in battle, the enemy realized the dead man was not a common person, and the corpse was treated well.

helmets, their *sashimono*, their flags, their horses' harness, and even on the minor parts of samurai armor such as the sleeves. On several painted screens, it is the Ii contingents who are the easiest to recognize.

Samurai Costume in the Edo Period

The final evolution of samurai armor occurred during the peaceful days of the Edo period when wars ceased. Suits of armor became prestige gifts, rarely worn during the long *sankin kotai* processions to and from Edo. Old styles were revived and modified producing some spectacular suits of armor that would have been most impractical for fighting in. These trends produced despair among contemporary commentators who still believed that Japan had to be ready for war, and that her armor offered the best protection for a brave samurai.

In fact, armor was usually seen only on display in a castle, and samurai would wear the *hakama* and *kimono* noted earlier. For more formal occasions such as guard duty in a

have been worn by high ranking generals only, a practice common to many families. Also, any color displayed on a suit of armor would have come about as a result of the shade that was chosen for the silken cords that held the individual scales of the composite armor plate together. It was only during the sixteenth century that armor was introduced that consisted of larger metal plates that could be lacquered and given a distinctive color of their own. The Ii adoption of red coincided with the start of the almost universal use of plate armor, and the way they expressed themselves was quite unique. In place of the usual black or brown lacquer for armor plates (and the very rare instances of individuals such as Tokugawa Ieyasu appearing all in gold), Ii Naomasa made glowing red the hallmark of his retainers. The color appeared on their body armor, their

Left: The stunning effect produced by red lacquer on one of the helmets of the Ii family's "Red Devils."

Left: Ii Naomasa, the *daimyo* of Hikone, who fought for Tokugawa Ieyasu at the battle of Sekigahara in 1600.

himo was the use of *mon* (badges) stenciled on to the front straps of the *kataginu,* the middle of the back of the *kataginu,* the sleeves of the kimono, and the top rear of the *hakama.* Alternatively, a looser jacket called a *haori* could be worn instead of the *kataginu.* The *haori* would hang over the sword scabbard, giving the samurai a characteristic appearance as he walked along. Contemporary illustrations also show the short *kobakama* being worn by men on foot on the *sankin kodai,* the regular trips to Edo which the *daimyo* were required to make to pay their respects to the shogun.

On very formal occasions such as an actual presentation to the shogun, a *daimyo* would be expected to wear the *nagabakama.* These were extremely long trousers that trailed on the floor behind the wearer. It was considered a mark of good breeding simply to be able to move in them, a feat which required supreme coordination. It also ensured that a samurai wearing *nagabakama* would find it impossible to perform an assassination, or at the very least to run away afterward (see page 133).

One important aspect of the samurai's appearance was the dressing of the hair, a matter upon which much care and attention was lavished. To even the lowliest samurai, having a single hair out of place was a disgrace. Woodblock prints often make this point by showing the desperate and defeated samurai in battle with his disheveled hair streaming in the wind. It became customary during the early sixteenth century to shave off the hair from the front part of the head. This had originally been intended to provide comfort when wearing a

Above: A theatrical print showing the actor Ichikawa Danjuro VII in the role of Banzuin Chobe'e. The typical samurai hairstyle with the shaved front portion of the head is well depicted, but Chobe'e was not in fact a samurai, but the leader of the *otokodate* (chivalrous fellows) of Edo, the townsman gangs. Chobe'e was eventually murdered in a bathhouse.

castle, the samurai would augment the *hakama* with a jacket called the *kataginu,* thus making a combination costume called a *kamishimo* (upper and lower). The *kataginu* was a curious form of jacket with no sleeves, in which the shoulder and back were quilted and stiffened so that they stood out like wings. The *kataginu* would be of the same color as the *hakama,* thus making a distinctive uniform that contrasted with the hues of the kimono beneath. A decorative, yet very important feature of the *kamis*

Left: A samurai's servant wearing clothing typical of the Edo period as shown by an actor at the Toei-Uzumasa Film Studios in Kyoto.

Far left: A *daimyo* of the Edo period dressed in ceremonial wear.

helmet, but by the end of the century it had become a mere whim of fashion. The tonsured portion of the head was called the *sakayaki,* and what hair remained was drawn back into a *motodori* (queue or pigtail) on the back of the head.

There were two ways of making this queue. One was called *chasen gami,* because of a fanciful resemblance to the bamboo tea whisk used in the Japanese tea ceremony. It involved coiling a piece of string round and round the lower half of the *motodori* so as to make it stick out in a tuft like a shaving brush.

The other style, which was more common, was to gather the oiled hair into a long narrow cylindrical queue at the back of the head, bend it forward and then back again, and tie it in place. This style was called *mitsuori,* or three-

fold. A variation on this style was called *futat-suori,* where the queue was bent forward only over the *sakayaki.* The end of the queue, however it was made, would be neatly trimmed with a razor. Young samurai, however, did not trim the forelock. This unshaven part was trimmed to make a triangular shape, and was regarded as a feature of great beauty among young boys.

Some samurai did not shave the head at all, but had all their hair combed back. Tokugawa Ieyasu spoke against this practice because he reckoned it spoiled the look of a head when it was cut off! In the same vein he praised Kimura Shigenari, because he had perfumed his hair, and this had made his severed head a more attractive trophy when Ieyasu inspected it after the battle of Osaka in 1615.

CHAPTER 5

edged weapons

*No samurai would
ever be without a sword
either in armor or in
civilian clothes.*

Right: A samurai swordsman in
"civilian dress" from a print by
Yoshitoshi.

Opposite page: A samurai swordsman is caught in the rain.

The Sword

No weapon is more closely associated with the Japanese samurai than the sword. It became known as the "soul of the samurai," and surely no edged weapon in history has ever been surrounded with such a wealth of mystique and tradition. Many of the swordsmiths themselves achieved legendary status, such as the famous Masamune and the equally renowned Muramasa, whose blades acquired a reputation for bad luck among the Tokugawa family.

No samurai would ever be without a sword either in armor or in civilian clothes, and a sword forged by a celebrated master was one of the most prized gifts that a warrior could receive from an appreciative *daimyo*. Yet much of the lore surrounding Japanese swords is of comparatively late origin. For most of samurai history, the primary weapons of choice for the battlefield were the bow and then the spear. It was only when wars had ceased that the sword acquired the reputation that it has today as the deadliest of all weapons. Fed by stories of wandering swordsmen and their duels to the death, the concept of the all-powerful samurai sword began to reign supreme. It was both weapon and symbol, forged as a religious act and wielded with superhuman skill in a way that the battlefields of the sixteenth century, with their firearms and hedges of spearmen, had seldom witnessed.

As noted earlier, the first swords wielded by the Yamato soldiers were straight-bladed weapons. These swords were carried in scabbards covered in sheet copper and decorated with punched designs. Some had a hilt ending in a bulbous, slanting pommel of copper, the "mallet-headed sword," while others, called the "Korean sword" had ring-shaped pommels, occasionally enclosing silhouettes of animal designs. The lengths of these weapons varied between just under 23 inches (60cm) to 47 inches (120cm) and 35 inches (90cm) was the average size.

The curved sword was first associated with the *emishi,* but it was not long before the advantages of a weapon that could be used f or slashing as well as thrusting became apparent. The result was the *tachi,* the classic samurai sword slung from the belt with its cutting edge downward. Two hands would be needed to draw it, so the samurai would present his bow to an attendant before going into action with a sword. The *katana* was the name given to the later form of sword, which differed little from the *tachi* in overall shape, but was worn in civilian dress thrust through the belt with the cutting edge uppermost. This enabled the swordsman to draw the sword and theoretically deliver a killing blow in one stroke. Another sword, the shorter *wakizashi,* was added from the sixteenth century onward, and was put through the belt with the *katana* so that both handles protruded upward. The pair of swords was called a *daisho,* and would have matching scabbards and fittings. When in armor, the *katana* would be slung *tachi*-style with its blade downward, and held in a leather pad. The *wakizashi* would not be worn in armor, and would be replaced by a *tanto* (dagger).

The first swords wielded by the Yamato soldiers were straight-bladed weapons.

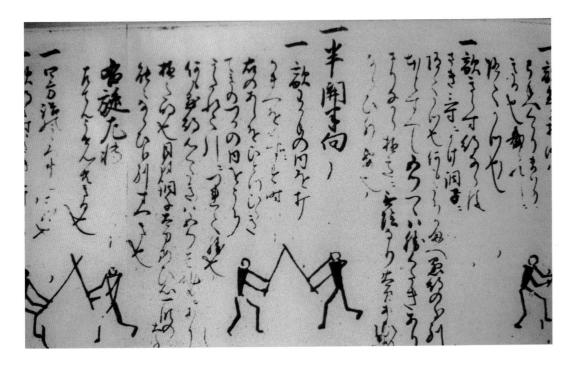

Left: Sword fighting techniques are illustrated here on a scroll preserved in the temple associated with the Yagyu clan's sword fighting school of the Yagyu Shinkage-ryu.

Sword Making

The making of a Japanese sword represented the application of techniques learned through centuries of practice and passed on from one master to his successor, demonstrating a knowledge of metallurgy that none of the swordsmiths would have been able to describe in scientific terms. Rather than being just one piece of metal, the Japanese sword was of duplex construction and consisted of a selectively hardened cutting edge embedded within a softer and springier body to give resilience. The early makers were probably iron smelters as well as swordsmiths, and would produce the materials required from iron ore mixed with crushed charcoal and heated by the burning of charcoal. The smelting operation lasted for four days, at the end of which the furnaces were broken up and the metal extracted.

The lump of crude iron so produced, called *tama hagane,* would be heated and flattened under a hammer, to produce a number of flattened platelets. A pile of these plates, coated with a flux made from clay and powdered whetstone in a thin slurry, would be forged out into a heavier piece of steel as a sword bar of about 5x6 inches (12x14cm) and about 1½ inches (2cm) thick. The hard tool steel for the sword edge and outer zone was called *uagane.* The *shingane* (soft iron core) was produced in a similar manner, except that it was exposed more often and longer to the air at a high temperature so that it would lose almost all of its carbon. When a pile of platelets had been forged to a single solid plate it was deeply grooved, folded over, beaten, and again hot forged so the surfaces welded tightly together.

Such folding and reforging was repeated, with the traces of the original pieces becoming

Above: Yagyu Muneyoshi, the founder of the Yagyu Shinkage-ryu, the most celebrated school of sword fighting in Japan.

steel, each welded and doubled five times to make 2^{20} laminations, or 2,097,152 layers. The swordsmith was now in a position to combine the laminated steel for the core and quench-hardening tool steel for the exterior. The simplest way was to weld a piece of *shingane* material on to a plate of *uagane,* the former being slightly smaller to ensure that it was fully enclosed, and then to fold the two-layered material together with the soft steel inside. Another method was to insert a bar of soft tool steel into a forged U-shaped trough of tool steel and then to close it and thereafter forge them. Some swordsmiths used more complex combinations. This bar, elongated on the anvil and fairly well shaped toward the contour of the final blade, was then slowly cooled (for softness) and brought to nearly its final shape by a kind of hand scraper that was pushed along the blade rather than being pulled.

When this process reached the stage where the only metal that needed to be removed would be what would come off when the finished blade was sharpened and polished, the most interesting process in the forging took place. This was the heating and selective quench hardening. In other words only part of the blade, the cutting edge, was hardened. To do this the smith coated the whole blade in a stiff paste of clay and water. The insulating clay was removed from the edge of the blade only, to a distance of a few millimeters. The remaining clay was dried and the whole blade brought to the uniform hardening temperature. This was a difficult process, particularly for a long sword. It was then quickly immersed in a

thinner and thinner. Two bars, one of *uagane,* the other of *shingane,* were forged in this way. It is thought that at times the composite bar was refolded sometimes longitudinally and sometimes crosswise, perhaps alternately. The great swordsmith Masamune used four bars of

trough of water "having the temperature acquired during the first lunar month." If the clay was well distributed and did not crack off, hardening was accomplished only within the desired zone, and in a pattern on the metal surface determined by the manner in which the clay was removed. Some smiths would choose a particular design of wavy lines as their keynote. The hardened blade was carefully examined, and if no cracks or faults were found the long process of polishing would begin.

The first stage of polishing was the removal of scale and metal, and was done by rubbing on a very coarse abrasive stone. At this point the curvature of the blade could be adjusted by heating the back of the blade and pressing it against a copper block. Polishing continued with a succession of finer grained stones until the final polishing was undertaken, a matter over which much secrecy was maintained. This would produce the characteristic wavy line known as the *yakiba,* where the hardened and unhardened steel areas met. The hardened cutting edge could then be sharpened to produce a cutting surface that was without parallel anywhere in the world, and the whole blade was mounted in a handle to produce the weapon that is so familiar today.

A *tsuba* (sword guard) protected the hands, while cord twisted round the handle gave a secure grip. Testing of swords was carried out to determine that they had the correct balance and would cut effectively. The cutting test was sometimes carried out on live bodies in the form of condemned criminals, but it was far more common to have the sword's power tested on corpses, or on bundles of rushes bound round a bamboo core.

Sword Fighting

Legends abound of sword fights being won in one stroke, of men cut clean in two, and of inferior sword blades being broken by a cut from one of superior manufacture. A good sword blade, it was said, should be able to do two very different things. First, it should be strong enough to cut through a pile of seven corpses placed on top of one another. Second, it should be sharp and sensitive enough that if placed in a flowing stream it would cut through a water lily floated downstream on to it. The most amazing stories, of which there are several varieties, tell of men being severed from shoulder to crotch so quickly and cleanly that they walked on for several places before falling in two!

This awesome and legendary power of the samurai sword derived in part from the curvature of its blade, which allowed the very hard and very sharp cutting edge to slice into an opponent along a small area, which would then open up as the momentum of the swing continued, cutting through to the bone. The other very important characteristic is indicated by the fact that it was a two-handed weapon, held by a warrior facing

Below: Kato Kiyomasa, one of the most celebrated samurai commanders, depicted in an ivory statuette. Note Kiyomasa's flamboyant helmet.

Above: A dramatic close-up of a sword-wielding samurai.

samurai to deflect a blow aimed at him by knocking the attacking sword to one side with the flat of the blade and then following up with a stroke of his own. Contemporary swords from other cultures would have broken if such a practice had been tried, a superiority in Japanese design that was first illustrated during the Mongol invasions.

As for the size of a sword, much depended on individual choice, as Matsudaira Chikuzen no kami (Kuroda Nagamasa's eldest son) commented:

> Weapons are things that depend on a particular person's abilities and preferences. Kato Kiyomasa was above the common run of men and possessed a surpassing physical strength. He wore a large suit of armor with items of military use tied at his hips, and carried a *tachi* up to a *sun* in width. Kato Yoshiaki, he of the similar name, was a small man and was in fact a weak person. He wore leather armor and carried a two *shaku* one *sun* narrow bladed sword. However Akai Hiza'emon of Shinsh was a weak little man but liked a heavy sword up to a *sun* in width. With this he once chased after a fleeing man, and cut him down from the top of his left shoulder to his right thigh. Again, Uesugi Kenshin of Echigo's samurai Nakamura Tajima was a big man with a big sword, but wore a papier-mâché armor and preferred a slender shafted spear, and performed great achievements on several occasions.

squarely on to his opponent. The samurai never used shields. Instead the *katana* became both sword and shield, providing a unique example of a sword used defensively as well as offensively. Such techniques were not seen in Europe until the late sixteenth century, when rapier styles evolved to include blocking and parrying as well as thrusting and the buckler was abandoned. This defensive use depended upon the immense strength and resilience of the sword's body and its broad back, which enabled the

Left: The *dojo* (practice hall) of the Yagyu Shinkage-ryu in Yagyu Village.

Sword fighting from a horse was not easy, because the normally two-handed katana had to be used in one hand. Any disadvantage in the strength of the swing of the blade, however, was overcome by the samurai's position above a foot soldier, and the momentum of his horse. The curved blade of the *katana* would cut into a small area of the opponent and would naturally be opened up as the forward movement of the horseman carried it along. In comparison with the samurai sword, a European knight's sword was dull and clumsy. A downward stroke from a crusader's blade might stun an opponent sufficiently to allow the knight to finish him off with a straight thrust. A samurai sword would do far more damage on the initial contact.

If there was time to dismount successfully from a fallen horse, some excellent swordplay could be seen from samurai whose desire to survive overcame any disadvantages that were posed by the weight or design of their armor. This is shown in this account at the battle of Shinowara in 1183:

> Arikuni, having penetrated very deeply into the ranks of the foe, had his horse shot from under him, and then while he was fighting on foot, his helmet was struck from his head, so that he looked like a youth fighting with his long hair streaming in all directions. By this time his arrows were exhausted, so he drew his sword and laid about him mightily, until, pierced by seven or eight shafts, he met his death still on his feet and glaring at his enemies.

During the naval battle at Mizushima in 1183, Taira Noritsune stretched planks across ropes to make a solid platform and some fine swordplay followed:

> And so shouting their war cry, they began the fight, drawing their bows and pouring in a hail of arrows until they came to close quarters, when they drew their swords and engaged each other hand to hand.

During the first battle of Uji in 1180, one of the warrior monks showed that he was familiar with several styles of sword fighting, by "wielding it in the zigzag style, the interlacing, cross, reverse dragonfly, waterwheel, and eight sides at once styles of fencing," he cut down eight men. But as he brought down the ninth with a mighty blow on the helmet the blade broke. That individual sword combat was still highly regarded as late as the Korean War is shown by this touching little anecdote of samurai comradeship from the battle of Sach'on in 1598:

> Zushi Sadakiyo went up to Izumi Shigeyasu, and said, "One cannot expect to wield one's weapons as one pleases when mounted, and in this present battle there has been no sword fighting at all, so let me take the horses for a while." Shigeyasu was very pleased, and replied, "There are no responsible people about, so I did not want to leave my horse here. I am deeply impressed by your honorable kindness." When he left his horse with Sadakiyo he advanced upon the enemy force and wielded his sword in great style. Truly, Sadakiyo's kindness was a thing one associates with a true friend.

During the fourteenth century Nanbokucho Wars, we find references that concentrate on the sword, such as:

> Although the three thousand horsemen of the enemy eagerly surrounded Tametomo when they saw that the warriors with him were a mere 20 men, the sword at Tametomo's waist was called Omokage, a three-foot blade made by Raitaro Kuniyuki, who purified himself for a hundred days beforehand. Omokage smashed to pieces the helmet bowls of those that came within its compass, or cut off their breastplates as though they had been monks' scarves, until at last the enemy no longer dared to draw near to that sword, but only sought to strike down Tametomo by shooting arrows furiously from distant places.

Sword Wounds

As for the wounds produced by swords, the battlefield situation made it a rare event for a man to be killed with one sweep of a sword blade as is portrayed in the duels at crossroads in popular Japanese movies, where the swordsmen wore no armor and had plenty of room to

Individual sword combat was still highly regarded.

maneuver to deliver the devastating stroke. In the press of battle the swinging of a sword was greatly restricted, and Japanese armor gave good protection. Of course, if a swordsman had the opportunity he could deliver a blow so powerful that it would split an opponent's helmet in two, but matters were rarely so straightforward. Historical records show that some samurai survived multiple cuts from sword blades. One victim was still alive after 13 strokes found their mark, and on a separate occasion a horse endured seven slashes. The siege of Namwn in Korea in 1597 provides a good example of both the power and the limitations of a Japanese sword. Okochi Hidemoto, "cut at the right groin of the enemy on horseback and he tumbled down. As his groin was excruciatingly painful from this one assault the enemy fell off on the left hand side. There were some samurai standing nearby and three of them struck at the mounted enemy to take his head."

Later in the same encounter Okochi was attacked by a group of Koreans and was knocked to the ground and, as he was getting up, several sword cuts were made to his chest, leaving him crouching and gasping for breath. His comrade Koike Shinhachiro came to his aid while Okochi parried five sword strokes with the edge of his blade. A sixth slash struck home, cutting clean in two the middle finger of Okochi's bow hand, but Okochi still managed to rise to his feet and quickly decapitated his assailant. Advancing more deeply into Namwn's alleys, Okochi soon encountered another strong man dressed magnificently in a

fine suit of armor on dark blue brocade. Okochi "was cut in four places on his sleeve armor, and received two arrow shafts that were fired deeply into his bow arm in two places," but in

Above: Miyamoto Musashi in classic fighting mode, holding one sword in each hand.

Right: The death of Imai Kanehira, who jumped off his horse with his sword in his mouth.

However, not all swords were of the superlative quality that traditional views would have us believe. Broken blades are frequently reported, and a samurai could also be put at a disadvantage when his sword got stuck in the body of an opponent that he had just killed. One warrior is recorded as praying that his sword might be dislodged from his enemy's corpse!

The sword could also provide an analogy for moral worthiness. For example, in *Hagakure*, Yamamoto Tsunetomo writes:

> There are two kinds of dispositions,
> inward and outward. And a person who
> is lacking in one or the other is worth-
> less. It is, for example, like the blade of a
> sword, which one should sharpen well
> and then put in its scabbard, periodically
> taking it out and knitting one's eyebrows
> as in an attack, wiping off the blade, and
> then placing it in its scabbard again. If a
> person has his sword out all the time, he
> is habitually swinging a naked blade.
> People will not approach him and he
> will have no allies. If a sword is always
> sheathed it will become rusty, the blade
> will dull and no one will think much of
> its owner.

spite of these wounds he managed to overcome the man and take his head.

The more lightly defended foot soldiers suffered more from sword cuts than the samurai. The grave pits of Zaimokuza, which contain the remains of victims of the capture of Kamakura by Nitta Yoshisada in 1333, show very clearly the effects of the Japanese sword on unprotected bodies. Many of the bodies are of civilians, and slash wounds to the limbs and skull appear on 60 percent of the male skeletons, 30 percent of the female skeletons, and 10 percent of the children. Most cuts were to the forehead or the top of the head, suggesting that they were delivered by mounted men. Some blows must have been of considerable force, because in certain cases the blade has bounced and cut again, or the skull has simply been crushed.

The Field Sword

The *nodachi* (field sword) was a sword with an extra long blade, and first makes its appearance at the beginning of the fourteenth century. Specimens may be seen in several Japanese

museums, but caution is needed before concluding that these swords were used for fighting, because many of the longer swords were produced by swordsmiths as offerings to shrines and temples. Nevertheless, there are enough references to the use of *nodachi* in the chronicles to confirm that long-bladed weapons were valued and could be used effectively by a warrior trained and skilled in their use.

Nodachi appear to have been used almost exclusively by warriors fighting on foot, and were particularly useful for dealing with a cavalry charge by breaking the horses' legs. Their long blades were often not sharpened for their entire length, leaving the area next to the handle blunt and rounded in the style called *hamaguri ha* (clam shell blade). The sword would then act like an elongated battle-ax. Use

from a horse, however, is recorded for Makara Jrozaemon, who fought during the battle of Anegawa in 1570. He was renowned for his exceptional muscular strength, which would have been needed to swing a *nodachi* from the saddle.

The Dagger

The dagger, or *tanto,* was a very important weapon for close quarter fighting, and throughout samurai history every samurai would wear a *tanto* in his belt along with his sword when wearing armor. At the time of the Gempei Wars, a session of individual combat would usually begin with an exchange of arrows, but when the two rivals came to grips it would be the *tanto* that decided the outcome on far more

Above: The site of the battle of the Anegawa in 1570, one of Oda Nobunaga's most celebrated victories. Most of the fighting actually took place in the river bed.

Above left: A priest from the Fudoji temple holds up a *nodachi* blade, which was considerably longer than a standard fighting sword.

Inomata immediately leapt upon him, snatched his dagger from his side, and pulling up the skirt of his armor, stabbed him so deeply three times that the hilt and fist went in after the blade. Having thus dispatched him he cut off his head...

Victory in single combat did not necessarily mean the end of the individual warrior's engagement in battle. He would usually continue fighting, as exemplified by a certain Kaneko Ietada, who fought during the Hogen Rebellion using his *tanto*:

Though both Takama brothers were noted for their strength, Ietada got on top and held Shiro, and was about to take his head. At this point Takama Saburo, in turn, dropped on top and, trying to keep his brother from being killed, pulled at Kaneko's helmet to face him up and tried to take his head. Hereupon Kaneko held down the left and right arms of the enemy beneath him with his knees, yanked up the left armor skirt of the enemy on top, and turning upon him, stabbed him three times as if both hilt and fist should sink into him. When he flinched back, Kaneko cut off the head of the enemy beneath him and raising it stuck on his sword point...

Above: The battle of Ichinotani in 1184.

occasions than the sword. At the battle of Ichinotani in 1184, the single combat between Etch Zenji Moritoshi and Inomata Noritsuna began with unarmed grappling techniques, and ended with a dagger:

The Glaive

The *naginata* (glaive) is the most common pole arm to be encountered in chronicles of the first

This sixteenth-century suit of armor is completed by the addition of a *kabuto* (helmet) and a *mempo* (face mask). The latter item provided protection for the face and also acted as a secure base against which to tie the cords of the helmet. His *katana* (sword) is slung from the belt and he has two *tanto* (daggers). His main weapon would probably be a spear.

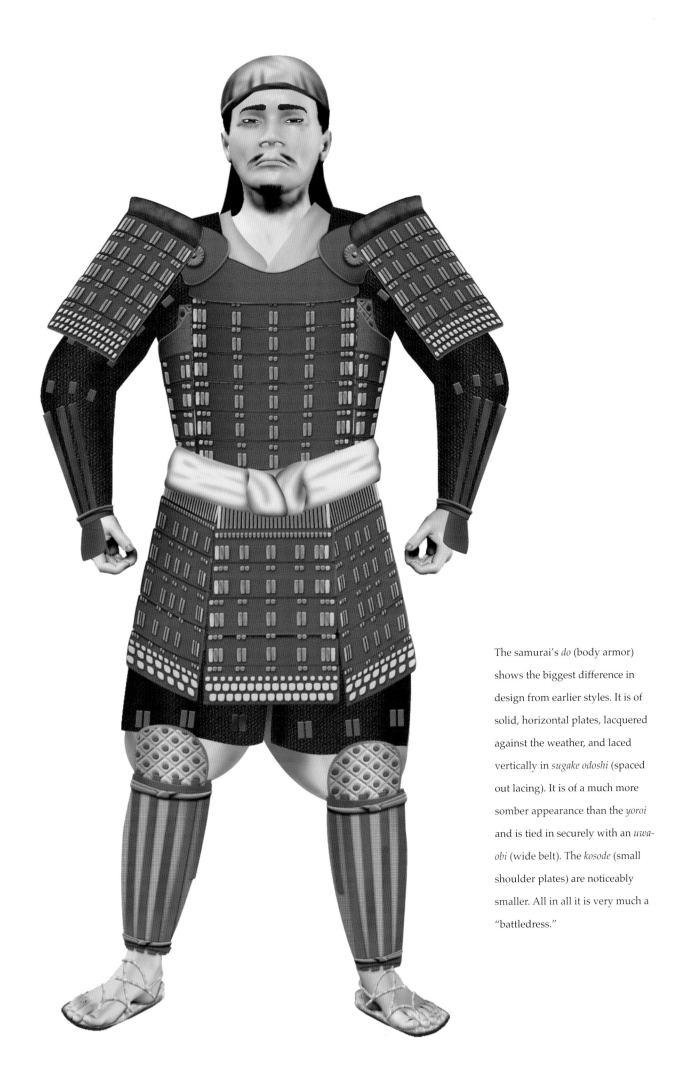

The samurai's *do* (body armor) shows the biggest difference in design from earlier styles. It is of solid, horizontal plates, lacquered against the weather, and laced vertically in *sugake odoshi* (spaced out lacing). It is of a much more somber appearance than the *yoroi* and is tied in securely with an *uwa-obi* (wide belt). The *kosode* (small shoulder plates) are noticeably smaller. All in all it is very much a "battledress."

The samurai is wearing two *kote* (sleeves). Each is a simple cloth bag with chain mail on the outside and metal plates at particularly vulnerable points such as the back of the hands.

The apron-like garment is a *haidate* (thigh protector). It consists of a heavy cloth backing on to which are sewn metal plates and chain mail. The *haidate* fastens behind the thighs and around the waist. His *suneate* (shinguards) are lightweight items with narrow, metal plates and a leather patch to avoid rubbing the horse's stirrups. The rest of the *suneate* are made from sections of cloth reinforced with metal.

In these plates we see the samurai in the most developed form of Japanese armor. It is practical and robust, and in keeping with its serviceable nature, he wears a simple kimono underneath it, on top of the undergarments shown previously. The kimono is tied in at the waist with an *obi* (belt).

Right: The blade of a typical *naginata*, the favorite weapon of the warrior monks.

few centuries of samurai warfare. It consisted of a blade with a pronounced curve mounted on to a stout wooden shaft, and was similar to the contemporary Chinese halberds, which had much wider and heavier blades. Although some samurai used *naginata* from the saddle, they were chiefly issued to foot soldiers. It was the *sohei* (warrior monks), however, who were to be particularly associated with this weapon, and one well-known account of *naginata* fighting occurs during the first battle of Uji in 1180, when a monk called Tajima:

> throwing away the sheath of his long *naginata*, strode forth alone on to the bridge, whereupon the Heike straight-away shot at him fast and furious. Tajima, not at all perturbed, ducking to

avoid the higher ones and leaping up over those that flew low, cut through those that flew straight with his whirling *naginata*, so that even the enemy looked on in admiration. Thus it was that he was dubbed "Tajima the arrow-cutter."

In the *Taiheiki*, there is a vivid account of a single combat between a sohei armed with a *naginata* and a mounted samurai:

> Just then a monk kicked over the shield in front of him and sprang forward, whirling his *naginata* like a water wheel. It was Kajitsu of Harima. Kaito received him with his right arm, meaning to cut down into his helmet bowl, but the glancing sword struck down lightly from Kajitsu's shoulder plate to the cross-stitching at the bottom of his armor. Again Kaito struck forcefully, but his left foot broke through its stirrup, and he was likely to fall from his horse. As he straightened his body, Kajitsu thrust up his *naginata*, and two or three times drove its point quickly into his helmet. Kaito fell off his horse, pierced cleanly through the throat. Swiftly Kajitsu put down his foot on Kaito's armor, seized his side hair, and cut off his head, that he might fix it to his *naginata*.

In experienced hands the *naginata* was a very versatile weapon with which one could beat, stab, and slash one's opponent. The *Taiheiki* relates how the monks were "whirling their great four *shaku* long *naginata* like water

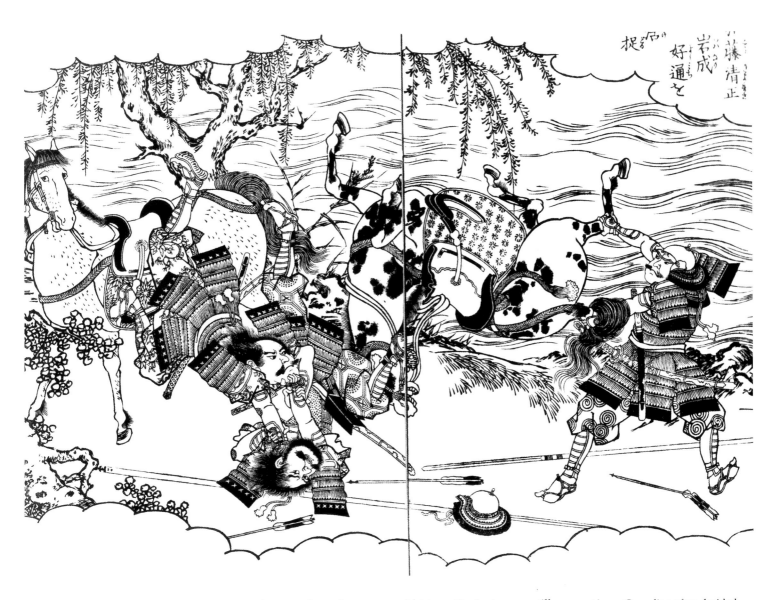

捉らへ々

岩成
好通を

加藤清正

wheels," the same technique used by Tajima the arrow-cutter. "Again and again they leaped and attacked with flying sparks of fire. Many were the warriors whose horses' legs were cut when they sought to smite these two. Many were those who fell to the ground and perished with smashed helmets!"

The *naginata's* flexibility of use made it a good individual weapon rather than one for massed ranks of infantry, as shown by the continued use of it by individual warriors throughout samurai history. *Naginata* were still to be found in use by samurai as late as 1598, when Reizei Motomitsu wielded one during the siege of Ulsan in Korea. Remarkably, the description of him "swinging his *naginata* like a water wheel" is almost identical to the ones from Uji four centuries before and also in the *Taiheiki*. The account of Ulsan in *Taikoki* tells how Reizei, "wielded his *naginata* like a water wheel, slaying 15 or 16 of the nearby enemy, before being cut down himself," although this

Above: Grappling often decided the outcome of a single combat, but in this example the victorious samurai has performed a *jujitsu* move on a horse!

Right: A samurai, charging forward on his horse, spears a Chinese warrior during a battle of the Korean invasion.

may be simply poetic homage to the glories of centuries past, using an expression that would be immediately recognizable to a reader.

The Battle-Ax and the Mace

Accounts of warriors using battle-axs are rare, but such weapons did exist and pictures of them appear in some of the oldest painted scrolls. The *Taiheiki* describes a certain Akamatsu Ujinori using one to "crush the helmets of several warriors" until someone cut through its wooden handle. Huge wooden maces, studded with blunt-headed nails, also appear, as do some weird and wonderful striking weapons with hooks and claws instead of a blade. One version was called the *kumade,* and during the Gempei Wars, one samurai received a blow from a long-shafted *kumade* on the top

of his helmet. The claws dug in, but before the foot soldier who had struck him was able to drag him off his horse, the samurai chopped through the shaft with his sword, and rode off with a new and unusual helmet crest.

The Spear

The straight spear, or *yari,* first appeared as an infantry weapon during the fifteenth century, and within a hundred years different varieties became the favored weapons for both mounted samurai and foot soldiers. Although by no means as versatile as the *naginata,* the *yari* was ideal for the tight and busy conditions of a battlefield where movement was restricted anyway. The samurai's *yari,* usually called a *mochi yari* (held spear), would be no more than 13 feet (4m) long.

Some illustrations suggest that the spears were used as lances from the saddle, others that they were more used for slashing strokes while standing up in the stirrups. The preferred option in attacking another mounted samurai with one's spear was to have the opponent on one's left. The spear would be held with the right hand across the body, while the left hand controlled the horse, but techniques were developed to enable the samurai to use this weapon in any situation: from a horse, in a charge on foot, or defending castle walls. Many of the painted screens that survive from the early seventeenth century show samurai spearmen on foot.

An interesting example of a samurai's *mochi yari* is preserved in Tokyo. It was presented to Hattori Hanzo, leader of the legendary *ninja* of Iga, by Tokugawa Ieyasu. Its original shaft length was 10 feet (3.1m), and it had a long blade (now broken) of originally 4 feet (1.27m). Kato Kiyomasa, another great general, favored a similar size of spear, but with a cross blade protruding to one side. Many *yari,* however, had comparatively short blades, which could be every bit as efficient in the right hands.

Above: Single combat during a battle is carried out by the hero Kato Kiyomasa.

Right: The set of *abumi* (stirrups) made of iron.

From the time when *yari* were introduced, they were used by foot soldiers as well as samurai. Their straight blades made them suitable for stabbing but not for slashing, unlike the *naginata*, but they could be as deadly. Hosokawa Yoriharu is noted in the *Taiheiki* as being killed instantly on receiving a spear thrust to his throat. A horse stabbed by a foot soldier's *yari* "went down like a stone." One other samurai reported that "I, Sahara Munetsura... was stabbed by a *yari* on the right side of my face as well as the elbow of my left arm."

Close formation infantry fighting, which became the norm from the mid-sixteenth century onward, favored the use of disciplined squads armed with *naga e yari* (long-shafted spears). The famous fences of Nagashino that protected the *ashigaru* arquebusiers were only half the story of that great victory. Standing beside them were hundreds of other foot soldiers armed with 16 feet (5m) long *naga e yari.* Waiting behind them were the samurai, ready to go in with spear and sword, and willing to defer their moment of individual glory until the moment was right in this classic illustration of the combination of arms.

Some historians translate the *naga e yari* as "pike," and Oda Nobunaga's use of *yari* with a 18 feet (5.6m) long shaft made them look like pikes. Yet, although there are obvious similarities between these weapons and the European pike, the traditions of Japanese warfare favored a much looser formation than was adopted by, for example, the Swiss. No Japanese battlefield witnessed the slow and remorseless "press of pike." Instead the *ashigaru* in the defensive hedge waited for cavalry with their spears at

Left: An unarmored samurai manages to fend off an attack by four armored men.

their sides. At the command they would take their weapons and receive the charge firmly. If a spear made contact their orders were to hold it in the wound, and only when the enemy was driven back did the defensive formation break up for a vigorous pursuit. Many *ashigaru* were also issued with shorter spears reminiscent of the samurai's *mochi yari,* and the blades came in several forms. Some have cruciform shapes, other a crescent moon-shaped side blade. The presence of side blades enabled them to be used for dragging a samurai off his horse.

After the initial exchange of gunfire and arrows, the samurai battlefield of the time of Sekigahara, therefore, would largely be a scene of spear fighting by both samurai and *ashigaru,* although some adepts would be seen whirling their *naginata.* If a samurai was seen using a sword, then it was likely that his spear shaft had broken, or that he was an expert swordsman who wished to demonstrate his skills. If two rival samurai were seen grappling then it would be probably the *tanto,* or even bare hands, that decided the outcome.

Deception could also be useful in single combat:

> To deceive the enemy, Tametomo feigned
> to suffer a wound, cutting his knee with
> a small cut and laying his body down.
> And then 50 unknown warriors came
> forward all together… and each thought
> to cut off Kageyu Saemon's head. But
> Tametomo made speed to rise up with
> his sword in readiness, saying, "Who are
> these that awaken a man when he naps
> wearied from fighting? Come, I shall let
> you have the head you desire."

CHAPTER 6

missile weapons

A samurai was known for being a mounted archer, not a swordsman.

Right: A samurai archer dressed in armor of the mid-sixteenth century. His quiver is slung at his belt.

Opposite page: A samurai archer sits guard, ready for action as always.

The Longbow

Many centuries before the famous samurai sword was being lauded as the "soul of the samurai," the Japanese warrior was being praised for his skills in *kyba no michi* (the way of bow and horse). In fact there are only two references in the entire *Shomonki* chronicle (which deals with the revolt of Taira Masakado) to the use of the sword. A samurai was known for being a mounted archer, not a swordsman.

The design of the traditional Japanese bow which the samurai wielded was very similar to that used today in the martial art of *kyudo*. To limit the stress on the bow when drawn the weapon had to be long, and because of its use from horseback it was fired from one third of the way up its length. To obtain the power needed in a war bow while retaining a cross section of reasonable proportions, it was necessary to adopt a lamellar structure, so the bows in the Gempei Wars were of deciduous wood backed with bamboo on the side furthest from the archer. Later on the performance was enhanced by adding an additional facing of bamboo. The rattan binding reinforced the poor adhesive qualities of the glue used to fasten the sections together, but as the glue could also be weakened by damp, the whole bow was lacquered to weatherproof it.

The arrows were of bamboo. The nock was cut just above a node for strength, and three feathers fitted. Bowstrings were of plant fiber, usually hemp or ramie, coated with wax to give a hard smooth surface, and in some cases the long bow needed more than one person to string it. Techniques of drawing the bow were based on those needed when the bow was fired from the back of a horse. In this traditional way the archer held the bow above his head to clear the horse, and then moved his hands apart as the bow was brought down, to end with the left arm straight and the right hand near the right ear. A high level of accuracy resulted from hours of practice on ranges where the arrows were discharged at small wooden targets while the horse was galloping along. This became the traditional art of *yabusame*, still performed at festivals. The archer, dressed nowadays in traditional hunting gear, discharges the bow at right angles to his direction of movement.

Among many incidents of skill with the bow and arrow, we may note the Herculean Minamoto Tametomo, who is credited with using a bow and arrow to sink a ship belonging

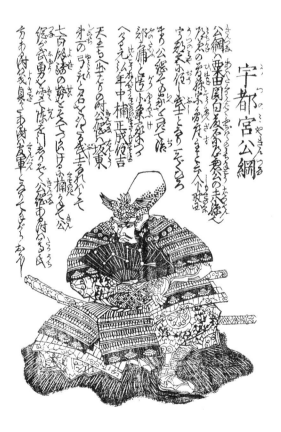

to the Taira by hitting it just below the waterline. At the battle of Yashima in 1184, the Taira hung a fan from the mast of one of their ships and invited the Minamoto to shoot it down, hoping thereby to persuade them to waste precious arrows. Nasu Yoichi hit the fan with his first arrow, even though he was on horseback in the water and the boat he was aiming at was rocking on the waves.

Nasu Yoichi's feat illustrates the fact that archery while wearing armor was a more difficult proposition than *yabusame*. The targets to be fired at in battle did not usually remain static, and the design of the armor also meant that the angle of fire was considerably restricted. The archer could only shoot to his left side, along an arc of about 45 degrees from about "nine o'clock to 11 o' clock" relative to the direction of movement. The horse's neck prevented any closer angle firing. The target, too, was not only moving, but also trying to kill you at the same time! Certain accounts imply that it was the power of an archer's shot, rather than its accuracy, which most impressed commentators, and Minamoto Yoshiie was credited with firing an arrow through three suits of armor hung from the branch of a tree.

Traditionally, every battle was supposed to start with an archery duel, and a set-piece battle would begin by the firing of signal arrows high into the air over the enemy lines. Each signal arrow had a large, bulblike perforated wooden head which whistled as it flew through the air. The sound was a call to the *kami* (the Shinto gods of Japan) to draw their attention to the great deeds of bravery which were about to be

Left: A samurai from the Utsunomiya family sits on a bearskin rug. His war fan features the constellation of the plough.

Right: A samurai with a longbow is represented on the vase on the right.

performed by rival warriors. The samurai would then commence a fierce archery exchange, with varying degrees of success, and then one or more feats of individual combat until the battle became general. The *Konjaku Monogatari* includes one very detailed account of a set-piece battle which involves a *yaawase* (arrow duel).

The encounter was fought between the rivals Minamoto Mitsuru and Taira Yoshifumi, who agreed to settle their differences in a pre-arranged set-piece battle. A suitable date and time was selected, and each turned up accompanied by a force of between 500 and 600 men. The armies were separated by about 328 feet (100m). After an exchange of messengers confirming the commanders' intentions to do battle, both sides started firing arrows at each other. But as the two armies approached,

Yoshifumi sent word to Mitsuru that they should fight a single combat. The challenge was accepted, and the two samurai fought a duel by shooting at each other from galloping horses. Fitting arrows with forked heads to their bows, they urged their horses toward each other, and each let off his first arrow at the other. After three arrows both considered that honor was satisfied, and the armies withdrew.

By the Sengoku period, the use of bows from horseback by samurai was a comparatively rare event. Instead the shooting of arrows by *ashigaru* supplemented the arquebus fire, but the bow was still prized as a sharpshooter's weapon by skilled samurai archers. It still had the offset handgrip, and was fired in a similar way. Alternatively, and more common with *ashigaru* on a heated battlefield, was a technique of firing a bow that began with the bow held horizontally and level with the waist. To release, the fingers supporting the thumb were relaxed, at which the bow, having discharged the arrow, rotated in the hand so that it ended with the string touching the outside of the bow arm. The use of bows by foot soldiers was in fact a process that happened quite early in samurai history, as the following passage from the *Taiheiki* makes abundantly clear:

> Now there was a kinsman of Akamatsu called Sayo Saemon Saburo Noriie, one who let fly arrows rapidly from a strong bow, and was versed in the fighting ways of outlaws… Stripping off his armor, Noriie made his way between rice fields and through thickets in the guise of a foot archer, crawled near the grand marshal behind a high path, and waited to shoot an arrow… But when Noriie had drawn closer and closer with his bow aimed, at last he pulled back the string to release the singing arrow. Nor did that arrow stray from its mark, but struck the governor of Owari in the middle of his forehead, just at the edge of his helmet. It smashed his brains, shattered his bones, and came forth as a white thing at the tip of his neck bone. And the mighty general's limbs fainted, so that he fell down from off his horse headfirst.

The reference to a "foot archer" shows that lower-class warriors were using bows by the mid-fourteenth century. Sayo Noriie was using a "singing arrow;" in other words an arrow fitted with a hollow wooden bulb behind the arrowhead. Such arrows whistled as they flew through the air and were used for signaling. The mess caused when a signaling arrow hit someone's face is well described in the previous passage.

Certain chronicles are able to give us a fair idea of the efficacy of arrows firing from the Japanese longbow. A direct hit between the eyes that avoided the peak of a samurai's helmet and any form of face mask he might be wearing, would of course be instantly fatal, but it was more common for samurai to die after sustaining multiple arrow hits. This was largely due to the stopping power of their armor, and the popular image from both woodblock prints and modern movies of the dying samurai crawling along like a porcupine with hundreds of arrows protruding from him is not too much of an exaggeration. A certain Imagawa Yorikuni, who fought during the Nanbokucho Wars, needed 20 arrows to kill him.

Some samurai were as tough as they were lucky, and one of the great heroes of the Gosannen War is said to have received an arrow in his eye which he proceeded to pluck forth and shoot back at the enemy! In the *Azuma Kagami* account of the Shokyu War, we read that, "Hatano Gor Yoshishige stepped out, he was hit in the right eye. His senses reeled, but he was able to shoot an answering arrow," yet others died lingering deaths from similar face wounds, or suffered the agony of having a barbed arrowhead withdrawn during field surgery.

Minor flesh wounds, by comparison, seem to have caused these fierce warriors little

By the Sengoku period, the use of bows from horseback by samurai was a comparatively rare event.

concern. An arrow went clean through the middle finger of Beppu Michizane in 1343, but two days later the same chronicle notes him being in the thick of the fighting. Four months later, however, the same Beppu Michizane was hit by an arrow in his foot, where the straw sandals offered no protection. The arrowhead could not be removed, so Beppu was forced to retire from active duty, and for the rest of his military career he acted as a guard at fortresses.

The Crossbow

It may surprise many readers to hear of crossbows being used in Japan, as the longbow was the weapon *par excellence* of the early samurai. It then became the exclusive weapon of the specialized archery squads of *ashigaru* of the sixteenth century. The crossbow did, however, make a considerable contribution to Japanese warfare over several centuries, both as the hand-held version and the larger siege crossbow which could fire stones as well as arrows.

The hand-held crossbow was the favored infantry weapon of the Han dynasty of China. It consisted of a powerful composite bow mounted on to a stout wooden stock, and was fired by means of a sophisticated bronze trigger designed to engineering principles of a very high order. The Chinese also solved the problem of the slow rate of crossbow fire quite early in their history by introducing a system of volley firing linked to a countermarch of alternating ranks. This was 1,500 years before Oda Nobunaga in Japan and Maurice of Nassau in Europe were to be credited with inventing similar tactics for firearms.

The high reputation that the crossbow enjoyed as an infantry weapon ensured that each attempt at army reform by the early Japanese included plans for conscript crossbow squads. The first appearance of the crossbow in

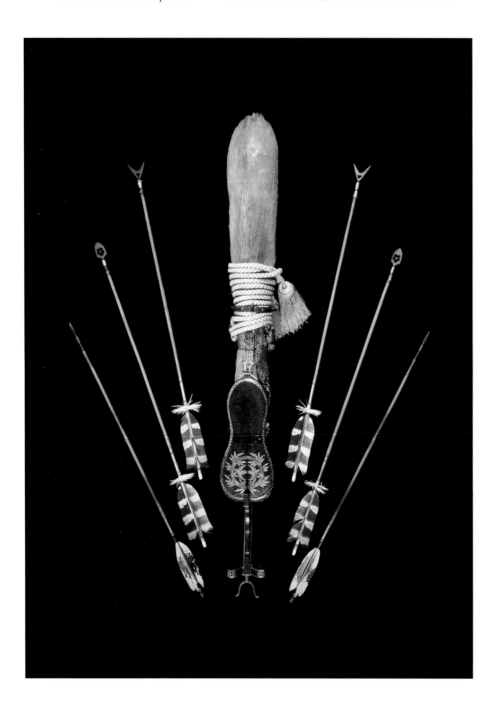

Below: A fine array of arrows set around a fur covered quiver.

Left: Various arrow heads.

Japan seems to have been A.D. 618, when the Kogury state of Korea delivered two Chinese prisoners of war and several pieces of military equipment. By A.D. 672, it was being used in Japanese warfare, with reports of crossbows shooting arrows "just like rain." During the 660s, when the fear of a Korean invasion was at its height, the Japanese government placed crossbows in a number of possible landing sites on the Sea of Japan coast, and the Taiho reforms of A.D. 702 specified the crossbow as an infantry weapon.

It was this reliance on the crossbow as an infantry weapon that proved its undoing, because as the use of conscripts declined so did the use of this particular weapon. The mounted archer needed the quick-firing longbow combined with a rapid movement by horse to demonstrate his individual skill, and when the conscript system was finally abolished in A.D. 792 following the humiliation of the *heishi* at the hands of the light archers of the *emishi*, the infantry crossbow effectively died with it.

The Siege Crossbow

The larger version of the crossbow used in sieges, usually called the *oyumi* in Japan, had a much longer life than the hand-held version, but as no specimen has survived it is difficult to appreciate either the size or the mode of operation of these weapons. Some Chinese siege crossbows were massive machines, firing several bolts at once and certain versions made clever use of a system of extra interlinked bows, so that the arrow was effectively being fired by two or even three bows. Certain records make tantalizing reference to the *oyumi* being

different from Chinese varieties, although this may just be an expression of national pride.

Descriptions of their use indicate that the Japanese *oyumi* do not appear to have reached either the size or level of sophistication of the largest Chinese models, but in A.D. 835 a Japanese artisan called Shimaki no Fubito Makito claimed to have improved upon the Chinese crossbow by producing "a frontier weapon" that "can be shot from four directions; it rotates and is easy to set off." This description is not unlike the Hellenistic tripod-mounted siege crossbow rather than the Chinese one that was mounted on a wheeled cart. In A.D. 838 the

government of Mino province ordered four of the new machines to replace 20 of the old issue, and in A.D. 894 there was a battle between Japanese and Korean ships during which crossbows were used. Whether these were hand-held or large varieties is not clear, but 29 static crossbows and 100 hand-held ones were among the plunder taken when rebels seized and burned Akita in northern Japan. There appear to have been two *oyumi* between each 50-man squad in the conscript armies that fought the *emishi,* and one account optimistically claims that "even tens of thousands of barbarians cannot bear up to the arrows of one machine."

In contrast to the predominant Chinese practice, the Japanese crossbows were used for throwing stones as often as for firing arrows. The historian Sasama has suggested how they may have looked, but his designs are so different from the well-established Chinese models that the simple addition of a wide enough sling to hold a stone rather than an arrow may well be all the design modification that was needed. In the *Mutsu Waki*, the chronicle of the "Early Nine Years' War" (1055–1062) the use of both arrows and stones is recorded, where "the assembled *oyumi* fired throughout the day and night, the arrows and stones falling like rain."

Stones are also implied by the use of the alternative expression *ishiyumi* (literally "stone bow") that is frequently encountered for the crossbow. In the *Gosannen Kassen Ekotoba*, which is concerned with the "Later Three Years' War" (1083–1087) the hero Ban Jiro Kenjo Sukekane is struck on the helmet by a stone from an *ishiyumi* and knocked to the ground, and in the

Above: This samurai on duty during the Korean invasion has received an arrow through his left arm.

The *ashigaru*'s helmet is a *jingasa* (war hat). It is in the shape of a lampshade and could be of either iron or leather. The *mon* also appears on the *jingasa*. A white head-cloth, effectively only a sun-screen, hangs from the rim. Around his shoulders are slung cloth-ration bags, each holding a portion of rice. His simple swords are thrust through his belt. This *ashigaru*'s weapon is an arquebus, a matchlock musket. The long fuse is wound around his arm, and he has a bullet bag and a powder flask slung from his belt.

The *ashigaru's do* (body armor) is of a style known as an *okegawa-do*. Quite large metal plates have been riveted together and then lacquered over to give a smooth surface. The *kusazuri* (skirts) protect the thighs in the absence of a *haidate*. The most noticeable feature of the *do* is the application of the *lord's mon* (badge or family crest) in gold lacquer on the front of the armor. This would have given the impression that one's *ashigaru* were dressed in uniforms.

The *kote* (sleeves) that the *ashigaru* is wearing are of very rudimentary design. They are merely cloth bags with plain metal plates sewn on.

The *ashigaru*'s first piece of armor
consists of a pair of *suneate*
(shinguards) identical to the
samurai's equipment.

The *ashigaru* (footsoldier) was the lowest rank of the samurai class. His costume and equipment were much simpler than those worn and used by higher ranking samurai. His undergarments are, however, similar. The trousers hold the *shitagi* (shirt) in at the waist.

本朝英勇鏡

和藤内
三官

Right: Kato Kiyomasa, one of the greatest leaders of samurai in the history of Japan. He took a prominent role in the invasion of Korea.

Osh Gosannen ki, which covers the same conflict, is a record of "a siege weapon" that fired stones from a castle wall.

The use of crossbows, with their technological sophistication and need for expertise in their operation, gradually declined in Japan in favor of mounted archery wielding longbows. There was also a political factor involved, because the resources of a centralized state were needed to keep this elaborate practice going, and as central authority declined through the Heian period so did the reserve of trained crossbow men. Crossbow adepts soon became hard to find, and one account of 914 laments the fact that soldiers did not even know the name *oyumi,* let alone how to use one. At the time of the Hogen Rebellion in 1156, Kiheiji Taifu was praised by his master Minamoto Tametomo for being

"one who can throw stones three *cho*" (about 350 yards or 320m), a skill attributed to no one else in his army.

The last time *oyumi* were used would appear to be 1189, when Minamoto Yoritomo led an army to the far north of Japan in pursuit of his brother Minamoto Yoshitsune and his Fujiwara allies. When Yoritomo attacked a fortress near Mount Atsukashi, he took eighteen heads in spite of many deadly shots from crossbows. But from this time on, references to Japanese crossbows disappear from the record. To some extent this was due to the fact that with the notable but short-lived exceptions of the Shoky War of 1220 and the Mongol invasions, the thirteenth century in Japan was a time of almost unbroken peace, giving ample opportunity for such a specialist skill to be lost completely.

Above: The samurai defending the coast of Japan march past the wall erected to withstand the expected Mongol invasion.

清正大石代を郷して明軍を破る図

Right: A huge rock is dislodged from the wall of Ulsan Castle to scatter a group of Ming soldiers during the siege of 1597–1598.

The Traction Trebuchet

The alternative to siege crossbows for throwing stones was to use the traction trebuchet. This was the forerunner of the more familiar counterweight trebuchet, which was never used in Japan, and instead of using a descending box of stones, the traction trebuchet's power was produced by a group of men pulling on ropes.

The exploding bombs flung by the Mongols during their first attempt at an invasion of Japan in 1274 were almost certainly launched from traction trebuchets, and it is more than likely that this was the first experience the Japanese had of either the bombs or the catapults. The *oyumi* was now forgotten, and although many long and lively sieges made up

much of the fighting during the Nanbokucho Wars, there is no specific mention in the *Taiheiki* of catapults. We might therefore conclude that no such machines were used, were it not for an abundance of references in war reports and casualty lists to samurai being killed or wounded by stones.

For example, in an account of 1341, there is a flag bearer called Hikojiro who "received a stone from Horigiri (castle) and because it broke his head he died." In various reports dating from 1333 onward there is mention of the flag bearer Nakabira being "struck at the base of the right eye by a stone," and another being hit on the shoulder by a stone as he broke into a certain castle. Another flag bearer is hit in the face "leaving him half dead and half alive," a dramatic expression also applied to a samurai struck on the head while he was destroying the water supply of Kaseta Castle. Nor are these activities confined to central Japan. In 1372, one of the Shibuya family fighting in distant Kyushu was "struck by a stone on the helmet so that he fell into the moat and died."

The circumstances of the example concerning the destruction of a castle's water supply makes it highly unlikely that this stone was simply dropped from a castle wall. The complex nature of the typical *yamashiro* fortress where these actions would have taken place makes a long-range traction trebuchet bombardment far more likely, but it is not until 1468 that there is an unambiguous reference to their use. In the *Hekizan Nichiroku* it reads:

A craftsman from Yamato province came to the camp and constructed *hassekiboku* (flying stone machines). At the place where the stones hit their mark they broke completely into fragments. The siege machines threw stones and devices like Chinese plums. The operators threw loads of stone or destroyed armies by spreading fire within their ranks. The strategy for these machines' operation was to shoot stones of twelve *kin* (16 lbs or 7.2 kg) in weight. They went about 300 paces.

The "Chinese plums" were soft-cased exploding bombs that exploded in mid air like a thunderclap. They had the shape of large ellipsoids

Below: Torii Sune'emon is taken in front of Nagashino Castle and told to shout that no help was on its way. Instead he encouraged the defenders and was executed on the spot.

Right: The castle of Hiroshima as it appeared before the atomic bombing of 1945. Hiroshima was the seat of the Mori *daimyo*.

and were fitted with a dragging handle and a wheel. A team of 40 men fired them by pulling on long ropes. The inclusion of fragments of iron or porcelain gave them the ability to cause injury, although their effects were by no means as serious as the iron-cased bombs used by the Mongols, the broken shell of which acted like shrapnel. Curiously enough, the Japanese never seem to have adopted this other variety of exploding device.

The statement above about the range and limited size of the projectiles illustrates how backward Japan was in regard to artillery compared to contemporary China or Europe, where even the counterweight trebuchet was reaching the end of its useful life but was still capable of throwing stones 20 times heavier over the same distance. It is also interesting to note that the stones broke up on landing, a matter which caused the attackers no concern,

so it is likely that the stones were being used as anti-personnel weapons in the classic Japanese manner, rather than for creating a breach, for which stones of greater strength than their targets would be required.

Sporadic references to stone-throwing catapults occur in the Japanese chronicles over the next two centuries, of which the most remarkable account concerns the siege by the Mori family of the castle of Takigawa in 1552. The defenders had prepared for the assault by collecting large smooth stones from the river bed and bombarded the Mori forces with them by catapults. The most interesting feature of the siege is that after the attack the Mori leaders compiled the customary list of dead and wounded, and noted the weapons by which the wounds had been inflicted. The list includes casualties from catapult stones, a feature unique to this document. Out of 181 men listed as

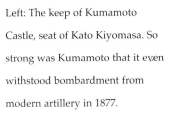

Left: The keep of Kumamoto Castle, seat of Kato Kiyomasa. So strong was Kumamoto that it even withstood bombardment from modern artillery in 1877.

Left: The Omote-mon, one of several very striking ornamental gates at the Toshogu Shrine, Nikko, built to honor the memory of Tokugawa Ieyasu.

wounded, 39 (22 percent) were caused by edged weapons when the two armies came to grips, while the vast majority (78 percent) suffered wounds from missile weapons. Of these, 142 in total, 108 (76 percent) were caused by arrows and 34 (24 percent) by trebuchet stones. In other words, the use of the traction trebuchet produced a nearly a quarter of all wounds from missile weapons, showing that its effectiveness as an antipersonnel weapon could be quite considerable.

Another very detailed account of the use of stone-throwing catapults in Japan occurs in the *Eikei Gunki* description of the siege of Mori in 1599. Mori, in the far north of Japan, was defended by a peasant army against an overbearing landlord, and their leader had "skillfully made from brushwood, [a term that probably means rough timbers] things for throwing

stones. Used by women and children, they could easily project them about one *cho* [120 yards or 110m]." Such a range, which is about one third of the distance the 40 foot soldiers of the Nin War could hurl their stones, sounds consistent with the machines being operated by untrained women and children, but the effect was no less devastating:

> Every single one of the two or three hundred women from inside the castle came out and began to throw down an abundance of large and small stones which they had already prepared, shouting as they defended, whereupon more than 20 men were suddenly hit and died. Many more were wounded. In fact, and regrettably, because of the women's act of opportunity in throwing stones, driven by necessity and scrambling to be first they jumped into the moat and fled outside the palisade. This treatment inspired those within the castle. (Then) about 20 arquebuses opened fire. This was not enough to frighten (the women), and the throwing of small stones from the shadows of the moat was like a hail storm. To the irritation of Shiyoshi, they struck Ishii Ukon Koremichi in both eyes and killed him. Similarly, they struck in one eye the horse that Kutsuzawa Goro was riding. Saying "to stay too long in that place and be hit by women's stones would be a failure bringing ridicule for generations to come," they returned to the original place of attack.

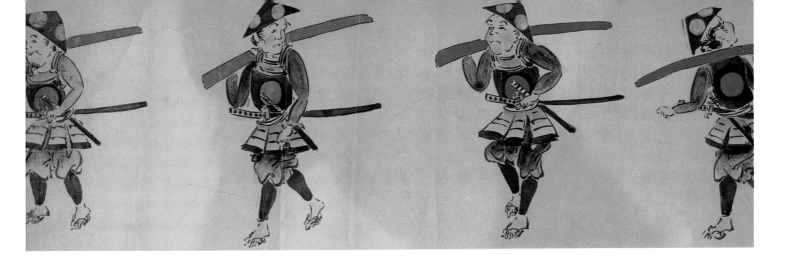

The traction trebuchet thus continued to be used in Japan long after it had been abandoned in China and the West, and a final reference to the use of catapults concerns the siege of Saka Castle in 1614, where Sadler tells us in *The Maker of Modern Japan* that the defenders installed "fire-projecting mangonels." This was the action when the Tokugawa besiegers bombarded the castle from a long distance using European cannon, so this remark, which probably has its origin in an observation by a European Jesuit priest inside Saka, tells us more about the shortage of artillery possessed by the defenders than about a reasoned application of defensive strategy.

The Arquebus

The Mongol invasion of 1274 is without question the first use of gunpowder in Japan, and it is a puzzle why such a militarily orientated society as Japan should lag so far behind China or Korea in the development and use of gunpowder weapons. Soft-casing exploding bombs fired by catapult remained Japan's only artillery until the sixteenth century, and it was not until 1510 that any form of metal-barreled gun was introduced to the samurai.

In that year, Hojo Ujimasa acquired a sample of a simple Chinese handgun, and although accounts of them being used in battle are rare,

Above: A file of *ashigaru* (foot soldiers) carrying their arquebuses in weatherproof lacquered cases. This is a painted scroll in the Shinshiro Museum.

Left: The use of arquebuses during a reenactment of the battle of Kawanakajima at Yonezawa.

Above: A vivid detail from one
section of a print depicting the
battle of Kawanakajima in 1561.

gunner needed both hands for steadying and firing, aiming was very rudimentary. In 1543, of course, there occurred the famous arrival of Portuguese traders on the island of Tanegashima, who brought with them European arquebuses. Within a few years these weapons had been copied, improved, and mass produced, and large numbers of Japanese arquebuses were being used in battle from 1549 onward. Chinese handguns were rapidly forgotten.

The first Japanese to fire arquebuses in anger were probably bands of pirates raiding China, and the fanatical monk armies of the Ikko-ikki were to be among the first users of arquebuses on a large scale. But the *daimyo* were not far behind, and it is no coincidence that the first of Japan's three unifiers, Oda Nobunaga, took an early lead in the adoption of firearms. As early as 1549, the same year that the Shimazu are credited with using arquebuses in battle in Japan for the first time, Nobunaga's father Nobuhide placed an order with the newly established Kunitomo gunsmiths for 500 arquebuses. In 1553, we read of Oda Nobunaga with 500 arquebusiers in his army, and the following year, 1554, was to see them in action at Muraki firing volleys by relays.

In 1555 another great *daimyo*, Takeda Shingen, sent 300 arquebusiers as a reinforcement to Asahiyama Castle, and guns like these played a large part in his epic battle of Kawanakajima in 1561. By then Japan had seen the first case of a general being shot dead by an arquebus. This had happened during the preliminary moves by Imagawa Yoshimoto against

the description of the battle of Uedahara in 1548 shows that their use had diffused from the Hojo family to other clans. These guns consisted of a short barrel and chamber with a touch hole to which a hand-held fuse was applied. A long wooden stock was affixed to the end, and as the

Left: The site of the battle of Nagashino in 1575, looking across from a replica of the fences behind which Oda Nobunaga's gunners sheltered.

Oda Nobunaga in 1560, and throughout the 1560s we find numerous references to arquebuses in all manner of armies throughout Japan. The battle of Nagashino in 1575, however, was to make a dramatic demonstration of how they should be used correctly, when Nobunaga detached 3,000 arquebusiers and lined them up behind a loose palisade, from which they fired in controlled volleys at the Takeda horsemen.

The Japanese arquebuses that won the battle of Nagashino for Oda Nobunaga took the technology of these comparatively simple muskets to its limit. They were loaded from the muzzle, and the burning fuse was dropped on to the touch hole by means of a serpentine controlled by an external brass spring and a sensitive trigger. A pan cover guarded against premature discharge. The use of standard bores, waterproof fuses, and prepared cartridges were Japanese innovations that made the arquebus the queen of the battlefield by the time of the Korean War of 1592–1598. In this conflict, above all, the superiority of mass volley firing of arquebuses over individual archers was demonstrated to no uncertain degree, and even in sieges the arquebus squads could be relied upon to sweep the Korean ramparts clear of the enemy prior to a devastating infantry assault.

Although the arquebus was predominately an infantry weapon, at one stage the arquebus almost became the samurai's weapon of choice, and there exists an impassioned letter from Asano Nagayoshi pleading that all troops coming to join him in the Korean campaign, including samurai, should be armed with guns.

However, the revelation of the power of the arquebus when used for volley firing worked against this trend, and, because the wheel lock pistol was developed in Japan after wars had ceased, the caracole of pistol-armed cavalry with which Europe became familiar was never seen on a Japanese battlefield.

Cannon

Firearms of a larger size, however, do not appear to have inspired the same enthusiasm in Japan as the arquebuses, and it is something of a mystery as to why this should have been. Japanese pirates (many of whom led respectable and influential lives back home) had been subject to Korean cannon for over a century, and on one memorable occasion in Japanese history a Portuguese ship was persuaded to use its firepower in a dispute between two samurai

families. This happened in 1561, when a Portuguese vessel bombarded the castle of Moji on behalf of the Otomo clan. The psychological effects on the defenders were every bit as serious as the very real damage that was done to their physical defenses, but instead of this leading to a cannon revolution comparable to the arquebus revolution of 1543, the dramatic demonstration seems to have been virtually ignored. Instead we read sporadic references to the use of cannon in Japanese sieges, but nothing comparable to the widespread and large-scale use of siege artillery that was transforming the face of European warfare.

The skills shown by the Portuguese in becoming gun founders in China was demonstrated in Japan when some guns were cast in Nagasaki, but the Japanese always showed a preference for ones made in Europe, and visiting ships were regularly lightened of their cannon as part of trade deals. At the siege of Nagashino in 1575, the defenders had one

Right: A short European cannon of the nineteenth century mounted on to a Japanese gun carriage in the Watanabe Museum, Tottori.

cannon, which they used to good effect in destroying a Takeda siege tower, but the Takeda themselves brought none. In 1578 the Otomo, whose Christian sensibilities did much to ensure a supply of European weapons, employed one Portuguese breech loader, identical to the Chinese *folang ji*, against the Shimazu Castle of Takajo. In spite of its impressive nickname *kuzurikuni* (destroyer of provinces) it failed to prevent the Otomo from being surprised by a Shimazu relieving army and being slaughtered in their thousands along the banks of the Mimigawa.

The siege of the Ikko-ikki, who possessed hundreds of arquebuses, at Nagashima in 1574 was accompanied by bombardment from cannon mounted on Oda Nobunaga's ships. These cannot have been very big pieces, and were probably of similar size to the swivel guns mounted on boats with which the Arima supported their troops on shore during the battle of Okita Nawate in 1584. Even the great Hideyoshi used artillery only for what reads like heavy caliber sniper fire, preferring to reduce his enemies' fortresses by fire, flood, starvation, or assault. The Hojo Castle of Odawara boasted many cannon during Hideyoshi's epic siege of 1590, but were unable to prevent its fall.

Most remarkably of all, when the Japanese invaded Korea in 1592 they took almost nothing in the way of a "siege artillery train" of any sort with them. Initially, at least, this optimism proved to be fully justified, as one Korean castle after another fell to Japanese assault accompanied by fierce arquebus fire, and it was only

Left: The grave of Ryuzoji Takanobu, who was killed at the battle of Okita-Nawate, near Shimabara, in 1584.

much later in the campaign that the invaders found themselves under pressure from Korean and Chinese cannon. This happened first from the firepower of Admiral Yi's famous turtle ships, but as cannon began to be used effectively from fortresses such as Chinju, the Japanese responded in kind, and mounted cannon, many of which were captured from the Koreans, on their *wajo* (coastal fortresses), which they then used to keep Admiral Yi's fleet at bay. Yet even these do not sound like artillery fortresses in the European sense, because in the records that exist of the breakdown of weaponry during the time of occupation between 1593 and 1597, cannon figure very slightly. For example, the *wajo* of Kadok, which had a garrison of 5,000 men, contained 200 firearms and 4,500 bullets, compared to 300 bows and 6,000 arrows, and of the

Right: A determined band of *ashigaru* (foot soldiers) lay down covering fire across the moat of Osaka Castle during the great winter campaign of 1614–1615.

guns 150 were arquebuses, and only one is described as being of "large caliber."

On returning to Japan certain commanders, notably Kato Kiyomasa, incorporated the lessons from Chinese siege craft into the design of their new fortresses, and Kato's great castle at Kumamoto shows an appreciation of the potential power of artillery. In fact Kumamoto held out against modern weapons in 1877 during the Satsuma Rebellion, but the most enthusiastic supporter of artillery as a siege weapon was Tokugawa Ieyasu, who became the first Tokugawa shogun following his decisive victory at Sekigahara in 1600. Cannon may have been present on the field of Sekigahara, but the wet conditions ensured that none was used. Instead siege artillery played a decisive role in several of the "side-shows" to Sekigahara

whereby Tokugawa opponents were overcome. In one case, that of the siege of Hosokawa Ysai's castle of Tanabe, we are reliably informed that so revered was the old man, who was a noted scholar and poet, that the Tokugawa forces bombarding his castle absent-mindedly forgot to put any projectiles into the barrels of their cannon.

Apart from a few bronze pieces cast in Japan, the majority of the Tokugawa siege artillery consisted of cannon obtained from European, chiefly Dutch and English, ships. The European terms "saker" and "culverin" appear in the literature, giving us a good idea of the size and range of these weapons, which were used to their most dramatic effect during the siege of Osaka in 1614. Prior to the siege Tokugawa Ieyasu bought up all the guns, powder, and ball that he could lay his hands on, and the Tokugawa culverins kept up a long range bombardment of Osaka Castle to which the defenders could not hope to reply. Instead of these modern European guns, the Toyotomi had only breech loaders—the ubiquitous Portuguese model again, and the "fire projecting mangonels" noted above, traction trebuchets firing soft-cased fire bombs.

With the establishment of the Tokugawa Peace, artillery became neglected once again and when the Shimabara Rebellion broke out in 1638, the Tokugawa army found itself with little in the way of artillery with which to bombard the rebels. They were reduced to enlisting the services of the Dutch, who obligingly fired a few token cannon balls at Hara Castle. The following year the Dutch demonstrated the use of mortars, but they do not seem to have been adopted.

Below: The Toshogu Shrine at Nikko, the mausoleum of Tokugawa Ieyasu.

CHAPTER 7

battlefield tactics

Many battles were carried out by surprise attacks, which involved night raids on buildings, arson, and the indiscriminate slaughter of all who ran out.

Right: Taira Kiyomori was a skilled samurai and also possessed consummate political skills that made him the pivotal figure of the mid-twelfth century in Japan. In this print he is shown wearing hunting gear, the same costume worn today for the martial art of *yabusame* (mounted archery).

Opposite page: The forward arrowhead of the standard battlefield formation known as *gyorin* (fish scales).

Early Samurai Battle Tactics

The history of samurai battlefield tactics is a story of interplay and conflict between two extreme models of army organization and deployment. The first model is that of the rigid, disciplined infantry squad, which makes its appearance twice, at the start of samurai history and at its end, in the shape of the Chinese-style conscript armies of the Nara period and the specialized *ashigaru* weapon units of the sixteenth century. The other model is the more familiar one of the mounted samurai archer fighting either individually or in small supportive groups, a pattern that dominated the mid-period of samurai warfare. Yet, at no time is either model totally absent from the scene, and the successful commander throughout history was the one who knew how to make the correct balance between them.

During the early years of Japanese warfare, the lessons learned from the experience of fighting on the continent were to be demonstrated as much in battle tactics as in the means of army organization. The initial shock of encountering cavalry for the first time had led to military revolution, and the defeat at the Paekch'n river two centuries later also caused much heart searching. The ultimate results were the conscript armies, whose battle tactics were dominated by infantry movements. In theory at least, well disciplined and heavily armored squads fought from behind rows of stout wooden shields, supported by mobile mounted archers.

This was the classic Japanese compromise between a conscript army and the use of elite mounted archers, as reflected in accounts of the war against Taira Masakado, when it is recorded that a strong wind blew down the line of shields. By the time of Masakado's revolt, however, the conscript system had been abolished, and it was the mounted archery arm that now dominated the battlefield, with foot soldiers playing a decidedly inferior role.

Most accounts of the time contain several references to what appear to be set-piece battles, most of which have an air of unreality about them. These would begin with the firing of signal arrows to call upon the *kami* to witness the brave deeds, and then a preliminary duel of arrows that enabled the samurai to exercise "the way of horse and bow" in the manner for which they had been trained. Large numbers of casualties are likely to have been rare during these "first round" fights, and we have already noted that one of the most famous archery duels of all, the one before the battle of Kurikara in 1183, was performed for a very subtle purpose. Minamoto Yoshinaka planned to divide his forces and surround the Taira army, but needed to cover these movements and hold the Taira in position. His solution was to conceal his maneuvers by fighting a prolonged arrow duel in classic style, a proposition the noble Taira could not resist.

In such a traditional set-piece battle one or more feats of individual combat would take place after the archery duel. The word used in the *gunkimono* (war tales) for single combat between samurai is *ikkiuchi* (single mounted warrior) fighting, which was to become the ideal for worthy opponents. Such a contest

The initial shock of encountering cavalry for the first time had led to the military revolution.

Left: Minamoto Yoritomo at the battle of Ishibashiyama in 1180. This was Yoritomo's first defeat, but he went on to win the war.

would traditionally begin with one warrior calling out a challenge in which he would recount at length his elaborate and honorable pedigree. This is so common in the *gunkimono* that it must have some basis in fact, but it is hard to see how a samurai could have much leisure for such a challenge once battle was under way, so it must have been largely confined to this preliminary stage. The proclamation would be answered from within the opposing army, thus providing a recognized mechanism whereby only worthy opponents would meet in combat.

The *Hogen Monogatari*, which describes the events of 1156, contains an excellent example of such a challenge, and also shows the importance attached to being the first into battle and how the heroic deeds of one's ancestors could make up for one's own lack of battle experience:

I am not such a great man as men go, but I am an inhabitant of Iga province, a follower of the Lord of Aki, and 28 years old. My name is Yamada Kosaburo Koreyuki. I am the grandson of Yamada no Shoji Yukisue, who was well known among the aristocracy for being the first to go into battle under the Lord of Bizen at the attack on Yoshihito, Lord of Tsushima. My grandfather also captured innumerable mountain robbers and highwaymen. I too have been many times in battle and made a name for myself.

Apart from recounting the stories of noble individual deeds of archery duels, challenges, and single combat, the *gunkimono* also contain many accounts which show how unheroic much of samurai battlefield behavior could be.

These sections, one suspects, represent the reality of warfare breaking through. For example, many battles were carried out by surprise attacks which involved the nasty business of night raids on buildings, arson, and the indiscriminate slaughter of all who ran out: men, women, and children alike. Most of the battles described do have some element of surprise built in, just to give one side an advantage. In such cases, the ends were regarded as justifying the means, and the otherwise heroic Minamoto Tametomo is quoted as saying:

> According to my experience, there is
> nothing so advantageous in striking
> down enemies as a night attack... If we
> set fire to three sides and secure the
> fourth, those fleeing the flames will be
> struck down by arrows, and for those
> who seek to avoid the arrows, there will
> be no escape from the flames.

Below: A saddle for a
samurai's horse.

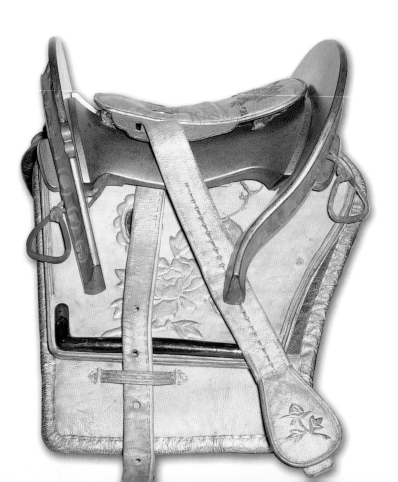

This same Minamoto Tametomo fought during the attack on the Shirakawaden in the Hogen Incident in 1156, which began with an archery duel in a surprise attack. His shooting was accurate and powerful, and he shot many arrows clean through saddles, horses, and his opponents, as the *Hogen Monogatari* tells us:

> The arrow pierced the breastplate of Ito
> Roku, who was first in the enemy's van,
> and passed through him, turned the
> sleeve of Ito Go's armor inside out and
> hung there. Ito Roku at once fell dead
> from his horse.... Tametomo shot before
> him and his arrow whistled through the
> air. It pierced the pommel of Yamada's
> saddle, and cutting through the skirt of
> his armor and his own body too, went
> through the cantle and stuck out 3 inches
> (8cm) beyond. For a moment he seemed
> to be held in the saddle by the arrow, but
> suddenly he fell headfirst to the ground.

Here we see an archery duel being used in deadly earnest. There is no formality involved and as it was conducted during a surprise attack at night, there can have been little in the way of a noble challenge about it. There were, no doubt, many good military reasons for such an approach.

When two experienced samurai armies engaged, both were likely to be similarly equipped and to catch an opponent off guard could be the only way of achieving any relative superiority. Samurai were realists when it came to winning battles, and a further graphic account of such an operation occurs in the

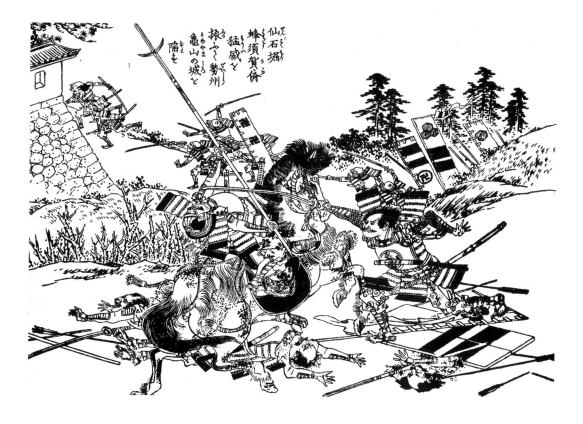

仙
石
堀
蜂
須
賀
侍
猛
威
と
振
ふ
勢
州
亀
山
の
城
と
陪
を

Left: Single combat between a mounted samurai and one on foot.

account of the Shokyu War of 1221 in a chronicle known as the *Azuma Kagami*:

> At lamplighting time the houses of the court warriors were all set on fire. As the flames spread, bringing destruction in their wake, the despairing and bewildered townsfolk ran wildly in all directions, afraid to live and afraid to die... Eastern warriors filled the neighboring provinces, seeking out foot soldiers who had fled the battlefields. Heads rolled constantly; naked blades were wiped over and over. Even on foot, it was scarcely possible to thread a way through the bodies of men and horses clogging the intersections.

Such accounts imply a huge discrepancy between ideal and reality in samurai warfare. However, it is important to note that these two different sorts of description actually occur side by side in the same story, with no implication that one is less moral than the other. The only way in which the samurai could be regarded as fighting in two different and contradictory ways lies in the very real conflict between individual glory and the needs of the group.

The notion of group loyalty in samurai warfare is as closely tied to their elite nature as is single combat and the seeking of a worthy opponent. Although the accounts of actual fighting in the *gunkimono* dwell heavily on single combat, the elite nature of samurai warfare did not depend solely on choosing a worthy opponent for one's individual skills. The

samurai had to be a leader, and the samurai commander had to be the leader of armies. His strategic skills in choosing ground, and the logistics of supply and recruitment, were all important to his success. But once the archery duel was over and battle had been joined, the fight became general, with a multitude of individual or group combats taking place.

In these situations the samurai tended to fight their own combats with little reference to their commander, who would not have been sitting at the rear controlling troops and surrounded by a huge bodyguard, as his descendants were to do, but would be in the thick of the fighting himself. His orders would have been given, and from that point on little overall control was retained, as he, too, sought a worthy opponent. The tenuous nature of the organization within the army also mitigated against chessboard precision. Samurai fought as units of individuals, whose reputations would be enhanced only by personal prowess. More importantly, perhaps, individual reputations would not necessarily suffer by the defeat of the army in which the valiant samurai had acquitted himself so well.

Fourteenth-Century Battlefield Tactics

During the thirteenth century, only the Shokyu War and the Mongol invasions provided any real military endeavor beyond a few obscure rebels. The Shokyu War was fought exactly like the Gempei Wars, and the Mongol battles were only different because their opponents fought

in foreign ways. The shock to the Japanese system of warfare that was delivered by the first Mongol attempt at invasion in 1274 proved to be just that, a shock. Once the second invasion had been disposed of by the *kamikaze,* the samurai could return to the mode of warfare they understood, of predominately mounted archers supported by foot soldiers, rather than the phalanxes of Mongol infantry. When samurai fought samurai there was no need to fight in any other way, and for the next three hundred years the samurai would be exclusively fighting their own kind, so battlefield tactics developed very slowly.

During the Nanbokucho Wars in the fourteenth century much of the fighting occurred during the defense of castles in wooded moun-

tains. There was still the occasional open battle such as Minatogawa (1336) and Shijo-Nawate (1348), but apart from these situations the accent was very much on defense where horses had a secondary role. Many samurai habitually fought on foot, and certain changes in armor, particularly the adoption of the foot soldier's *do-maru* style rather than the cumbersome box-like *yoroi* reflected this in part.

However, an analysis of the accounts of the period reveals that apart from such minor changes due to siege warfare, there was very little change in battlefield tactics from the time of the Gempei Wars, with any major differences being due to the terrain on which the battle was fought. Cavalry still easily overcame infantry when out in the open, and as one account notes

Above: Single combat between two samurai from horseback. They have discarded their bows, and are now fighting using their swords. Each is wearing a *horo,* the stiffened cloak often used to indicate that the warrior was particularly outstanding.

Opposite page: A samurai leaves a battlefield cradling the severed head of an opponent under his arm.

acutely, "foot soldiers may be strong, but they are not strong enough to stop arrows; they may be fast, but not fast enough to outrun horses." The mounted archers, naturally, preferred open ground on which to operate, and one reason for the frequent reference to arson in the accounts was the need to create such an open space artificially. The alternative was that sharpshooters with the bow might climb on to the roofs of buildings and pick off individual horsemen. For example, on one occasion some samurai horsemen of the Hosokawa were trapped on the edge of Lake Biwa and fired at from boats:

> They could not pass to the north because they had not finished burning the dwellings of *tsu*. A deep lake to the east was likewise impassable, forcing the Hosokawa army to advance in single file along a narrow road. The enemy rowed parallel to the Hosokawa and shot them from the side, killing five hundred in all.

It was only in situations like this when dismounted troops could hope to triumph over the mounted samurai.

Battle Tactics in the Muromachi Period

In the *Taiheiki* it speaks of "300,000 horsemen of the Kanto," but these are not for attacking inaccessible little castles. For this, it tells us, there was a change to group fighting. However, the Kanto force was responding to field fighting, but in mountain peaks, piled one on top of another, mounted men were at a disadvantage,

Compared with the samurai class, the lower rank ashigaru increased in numbers.

particularly when embarrassed by Kusunoki Masashige's unusual use of his followers as foot soldiers. After this experience armor, weapons, and techniques changed.

When heavily armored mounted men were defeated by lightly armored *ashigaru*, single horsemen were formed into groups, and we see the great change in the *Taiheiki*. In this period the *shashu no ashigaru* (*ashigaru* archer as the term is used in the *Taiheiki*) appears on the scene. A group of soldiers of low rank, they produced a barrage of arrows. They also performed light and fast guerrilla warfare, destruction, arson, and raids. Even the strong and brave mounted samurai was attacked by bare-limbed infantry. For this reason many *daimyo* began to organize raiding parties of *ashigaru* units. In the *Taiheiki,* for the battle of Shijo Nawate, "Sasaki Sado Hangwan Nyudo sent 2,000 horsemen up the mountain to the south of Ikoma... out of the men and horses 800 *shashu no ashigaru* were launched, and fired prolifically at the horses of the enemy." In other words, out of an army of 2,000, 800 were *ashigaru* archers, and these 800 flooded the enemy with a hail of arrows. Subsequently, the decreasing prominence of mounted warriors may be inferred from the existence of the firearms squads and spear squads of the later Muromachi period.

Further on, *ashigaru* as members of lower classes in battle were seen as essential, and the tradition of the horse riding samurai commissioned officer rank changed. Thus, gradually compared to the samurai class, the lower rank *ashigaru* increased in numbers. In the *Taiheiki,*

"that night, at about midnight, 3,000 *nobushi* climbed up the rear of the mountain, there were more than 800 *ashigaru*, they sent them round and raised the war cry."

Nobushi were not necessarily lower-class warriors, but was a term indicating what they did, i.e. they acted as skirmishers, not as massed troops or individual warriors. For example, "feigning retreat we lured enemy *nobushi* into open fields and our horsemen surrounded them. Fourteen *nobushi* were captured or killed. Of the 14, five were samurai, three with surnames were also captured alive."

Above: In one of his more audacious episodes of siege work, Toyotomi Hideyoshi is supposed to have used wood and paper to build what appeared to be an entire castle in one night. This so impressed the garrison of the castle he was besieging that they immediately surrendered.

Left: Yamaga Soko, whose contribution to the fighting arts was in the field of grand strategy.

Above: The taking of an enemy's head was an important element in the samurai ideal of warfare. Here we see it dramatically portrayed in a scroll from Ueda Castle.

With many *nobushi* and *ashigaru* being used, battle tactics naturally changed. Surprise attacks and guerrilla warfare flourished, and mounted men came to be less and less prominent. In the attack on Yamazaki in the *Taiheiki*, there is a reference to *nobushi* warfare, as this "strategy of elusiveness (*shinsutsu-kibotsu no sempo*)" became known, along with guerrilla warfare.

In the *Hojo Godaiki* we read, "In all the provinces of the Kanto they seized their bows and arrows and war was unceasing from east to west and from south to north. At this time guns

were few but bows were many.... They took note of a ranging arrow and fired bundles of arrows into the enemy ranks and disordered them. This was called *nobushi* warfare."

In the olden days, generals or high ranking samurai were dismayed if they had to command infantry, but this now changed. Also, from the Nanbokucho times, spears began to be used. They were handled with ease by infantry and used in raiding. Spear units were set up, and placed in the front line at a battle, which explains the expressions "*ashigaru* warfare" and "*ashigaru* battles." In the *Shogun Jizo Gunki*, in the chapter dealing with Hosokawa Ujitsuna's entry into Yodo Castle, it reads: "Miyoshi Nagayoshi gathered together the upper and lower units of Settsu and attacked Kawachi province... every day there was *ashigaru* warfare without ceasing."

From a later time, in the *Shinsen Nobunaga ki,* we read, "as opposed to 10 or 20 horsemen setting out together, there is only *ashigaru* warfare," which refers to light soldiers placed in the front ranks and used for *ashigaru* warfare.

Another expression is *ashigaru seriai* (*ashigaru* competition). The spear units were much used, as in the *Miyoshi ki* for the battle of Shari-ji, "From Miyoshi the first advance was against Hatakeyama Sashu and Matsuura Hizen no kami, and several hours of conflict ("spears coming together") developed. The number of spears for both sides in the competition was 900. It became a modern competition with no surprises."

So, at about the end of the Muromachi period, there were 900 spears on a battlefield. This surprised some people, but was the start of long-shafted spear units charges of later times. Then the benefits of spears reached even to the high-ranking samurai, and later spears were straightforwardly substituted for bows and arrows and became a samurai's preferred weapon. From this, of course, many mounted samurai too began to use them in units. As for charging with a spear, the use by *ashigaru* increased and samurai were enthusiastic for it. As samurai units gained more spearmen, military techniques began to transform as a result.

In the olden days, the samurai had a bow at his side. Now it was a spear, and we see as a result the use of the words from "thrust in a horizontal spear" rather than "thrust in a horizontal arrow" as an expression meaning to interrupt, from descriptions of a spear unit's flank attack. In the *Onin ki*, "Hatakeyama Masanaga, on his horse, raised his loud voice... and they entered the burned out ruins of the Fuko In with horizontal spears." So, up to the end of the Muromachi period, there were archery fights, then charging with spears by *ashigaru*, and after this the mounted samurai spear charges. In defense too, after the arrow fighting, the spears made a ring of steel when one was surrounded.

Battlefield Tactics in the Sengoku Period

Matters began to change with the large-scale wars of the Sengoku period. For a while foot soldiers were still the inferior arm, and during the latter part of the fifteenth century were regarded with some justification as being even more inferior than infantry had been for centuries. This was because of the introduction of *ashigaru* into armies. The name literally means "light feet," and originally *ashigaru* were no more than absconding peasants, thieves, and opportunists who joined an army, any army, for the prospect of loot. So desperate were some of the early *daimyo* to recruit troops that in many case men like these outnumbered their own foot soldiers whose families had served them loyally as warriors and farmers for many years.

With many nobushi *and* ashigaru *being used, battle tactics naturally changed.*

Above: The great "battle in the snow" at Mikata ga Hara in 1572.

With such a mob under one's control, battlefield tactics grew increasingly haphazard until the more enlightened *daimyo* realized that these *ashigaru* had to be disciplined and given the same continuity of service that his loyal troops enjoyed. Coupled with this was the need to have disciplined squads for the long-shafted spears and the arquebuses, and as the years went by more and more *ashigaru* units appeared on battlefields wearing simple uniform armor and fighting in organized teams. It was almost as if the Chinese ideal of the Nara period, whereby infantry fought in well-disciplined units of specialists, was finally realized.

The samurai, of course, still dominated the battlefield, but here too vast differences developed from an earlier age. The mounted archer could now be withstood by disciplined groups of infantry, so the mounted archer eventually gave way to the mounted spearman, enabling the cavalry to provide the shock of a battle in a way that their role as individual mounted archers had never allowed. The

Takeda family were particularly noted for their cavalry warfare, and at Uedahara in 1548 and Mikata ga Hara in 1572 they rode down disorganized infantry units.

Armies were now also much larger, and many battles tended to be fought between alliances of armies. Careful strategic planning, with the cooperation between separate clan armies facilitated by an efficient battlefield communication system, enabled the successful commander to control synchronized movement by units who were physically separated, so that each man knew his role in the current endeavor.

Instead of leading the charge into battle himself, the commander, seated, wherever possible, in a position where he would have the best overall view of the battlefield, would give his orders to his subordinate generals, who would transmit them down through the chain of command. Traditionally, the overall commander would sit in some state upon a folding camp stool within a semi-enclosed space provided by the *maku*, the large curtains bearing his *mon* (badge) which would be erected on site. The *maku* was such a feature of samurai life that the shogunate established by Minamoto Yoritomo was known as the *bakufu*, the "government from within the *maku*."

The transformation from an army on the march to an army in battle lines was facilitated by the existence of certain recommended battle formations, most of which were based on old Chinese models. All had some features in common, such as the general positioned to the rear center, surrounded by his bodyguard; the cavalry units ready to charge; a vanguard of

brave samurai and *ashigaru* missile troops protected by *ashigaru* spearmen; and a sizeable flank and rear contingent. The baggage train would be guarded to the rear. Different units would communicate with one another through the highly-mobile mounted messengers. Other messengers, some of whom would be on foot, would operate between allied contingents at different positions on the field.

One big change for the samurai was that tactical considerations now meant that the age-old honor of firing the first shot was almost invariably won by a lowly, and probably anonymous, *ashigaru*. The accepted tactical practice was for the first exchange of fire to be between the arquebus troops, firing at a maximum range of about 328 feet (100m). The firing would be controlled by the *ashigaru kashira* (captain) ordering the gunners through

Left: A group of samurai standing beside a *maku*, the large field curtains that concealed a commander's headquarters post on a battlefield.

Above: The troops of the Ii family, easily recognizable from their red armor and flags, go into action at the battle of Nagakute in 1584.

their *ko gashira* (lieutenant) under the overall direction of the *ashigaru taisho* (general of *ashigaru*). As he was probably in the most forward position of the samurai commanders, he would be able to judge when the firing had disorientated the enemy sufficiently for a charge to be ordered. At this point the *ashigaru* spearmen would advance, and the samurai would attack on foot or from horseback. While this was going on, the *ashigaru* missile troops would reorganize themselves under the protection of other *ashigaru* spearmen.

The battles of the Sengoku period therefore became a contest between the shock of a cavalry charge and the disciplined firepower of infantry, and the effects of the initial arquebus fire could make a tremendous difference to the outcome of a battle. In some cases, like the battle of Tennoji in 1615, with which the siege of Osaka concluded, troops were forced into precipitate action by arquebus fire. At Mikata ga Hara in 1572, the lack of protection given to the arquebusiers meant that they were overrun. In the most famous case of all, that of the

Takeda at Nagashino in 1575, mounted samurai were almost broken by gunfire, but it is important to remember that many hours of fierce hand-to-hand fighting followed before the battle was over.

Oda Nobunaga's use of three ranks of rapid volley firing at Nagashino does not seem to have been repeated very often. This may be because the concentration needed by his gunners was facilitated by the defense works. In most cases, two ranks of fire seems to have been the maximum possible. Any gap in the rhythm was made up by the archers, and several contemporary illustrations show a smaller number of archers standing beside the arquebusiers, while the spearmen stand ready to form a defensive hedge. *Ashigaru* archers were used for skirmishing and also in the firing line, where they filled in the gaps between arquebus firing.

On many occasions samurai chose to dismount and fight on foot in infantry formations. Few samurai were too proud to risk the outcome of a battle for their own glory, yet, whatever sophisticated battlefield tactics existed at this late stage in samurai history, the ideal was still what it had been during the Gempei Wars: to be the first into battle, and to take the head of a worthy opponent. At Gifu in 1600, two commanders almost came to blows over who should lead the attack, a matter that was resolved by one agreeing to attack the front gate while the other assaulted the rear. As a result, for every description in the chronicles of, say, the Korean War of 1592–1598 that describe a samurai general painstakingly arranging his

arquebus squads, there are a dozen describing individual combat in a way that would not have disgraced the hyperbole of the *Heike Monogatari*. An example is the battle of Yong'in in Korea in 1592:

> Ten thousand enemy soldiers had drawn up their ranks on a low hill. The gap between Yasuharu and the enemy was 17–18 *cho* from Yong'in. They put out the flags, and his family member Yamaoka Sakin charged ahead of the others so that he could engage in single combat. When the enemy ranks saw this there was great fear. We saw that a few wavered. From inside the castle too Wakizaka's banners were seen as they galloped out, making those inside and those outside become as one. As day began they cut their way into the enemy ranks with an enthusiastic assault and advanced into the enemy ranks. Seeing them being driven back down the rear of the hill, Yasuharu waved his fan for them to ascend the hill and take the enemy lines, and all their forces were stranded because of our advance, so we were cutting them down far and wide. The enemy had immediately become a defeated army, and were driven back along the road toward Pusan. Some were cut down and abandoned. Some were taken alive. In the space of half an hour several tens of thousands of the enemy were destroyed by our little force. The victorious attack was reported to all the Japanese forces in Korea.

The battles of the Sengoku period became a contest between the shock of a cavalry charge and the disciplined firepower of infantry.

Yet no commander underestimated the importance of *ashigaru* firepower, as shown by the use of arquebuses during the retreat from P'yngyang in 1593:

> Some time after the enemy crossed the river and attacked. Because it had been anticipated for some time past that the enemy would cross the river, when it happened they fired a volley from the arquebuses and after this raised the battle cry and charged forward impetuously. The enemy's attack was also violent, producing many injured men among our troops. However, although we were defeated in this episode, the enemy's large army followed up their victory by attacking repeatedly, and it is thought that not even one man of our small force returned alive. Because all present fought furiously toward their certain death, great enemies though they may have been, they were even split and pursued to the river before they defeated us. Our troops even thought that it was they who had gained the victory.

This was to be the mark of successful battlefield tactics in the Sengoku period which was a combination of arms, the discipline of the lower-class troops, and the self-discipline of the samurai, who had to hold back until the appropriate moment when they could finally attempt to emulate the exploits of their ancestors of old.

Stand-off at Kawanakajima

Sometimes battlefield tactics had to be used with great caution. In 1555, the Takeda main body advanced across the Chikumagawa and took up position across the Saigawa from Zenkoji at a place called Otsuka. Uesugi Kenshin marched down to oppose him, and on August 4, 1555 the Takeda and Uesugi fought each other across the Saigawa on the first day of an encounter that is known to history as the second battle of Kawanakajima.

There was no immediate result from the first two days of fighting, and the battle subsided into a situation of stalemate and cautious maneuvering that was to last for nearly four months. Throughout this time the letters of commendation and other correspondence issued by both commanders from the erected field positions make it clear that most of the fighting happened at places other than the banks of the Saigawa. Uesugi Kenshin launched one particularly furious assault across the Susohanagawa against Asahiyama, but Shingen's arquebuses proved their worth and no impression was made on the fortress. In contrast, two huge armies on the battlefield itself engaged in a series of skirmishes, but otherwise just glared at each other.

More than any other event in the 11-year saga of their confrontations at Kawanakajima, this second battle in 1555 has given rise to the popular image of Kawanakajima as a series of mock battles. There was some fighting in midstream as the vanguard of one army tried to entice the other to engage them, but each commander was waiting for the other to make a mistake from which some genuine advantage

Opposite page: Left for dead on the battlefield, the samurai Akechi Mitsuchika rises up from amid the corpses to continue the fight. This was the spirit of the samurai: virtually unquenchable except by death.

Left: Tokugawa Ieyasu, the founder of the Tokugawa shogunate. His effigy is in the family temple at Okazaki.

Right: The samurai Kakizaki Kageie, who led the charge of the Uesugi army at the fourth battle of Kawanakajima in 1561.

could be gained. The situation at the second battle of Kawanakajima was that of two evenly matched armies facing each other across a wide riverbed that gave them few advantages and even fewer opportunities. In contrast to the war of movement that had characterized the furious series of events in 1553, the war of 1555 was more static with both sides trapped by their own cleverness.

It is nonetheless most unlikely that the ordinary samurai encamped beside the Saigawa believed they were taking part in a mock battle. A better analogy is the situation in the trenches of World War I, which provides parallels to factors such as Uesugi Kenshin's policy for defeating boredom by launching raids every night. On one occasion Takeda Shingen responded by mobilizing over 1,000 men for a night attack on the Zenkoji position. This turned out to be a failure. Another raid consisted of an Uesugi attack on Shingen's supply train bringing rice from Kai. There may have been little of a decisive battle, but the four months of fighting were real enough.

In the end it was the demands of agriculture rather than the battlefield that prevailed upon

Above: The beauty of the traditional Japanese garden is illustrated here in an example on the site of the battlefield of Kawanakajima.

不識院大僧都謙信公

ふしきいんたいそうづけんしんこう

Right: Uesugi Kenshin, one of the greatest *daimyo* of the sixteenth century. He is shown clutching a length of green bamboo, more of a symbol than a weapon.

both sides to withdraw. These were the days when many samurai were part-time farmers too, and the *ashigaru* were urgently needed in the fields. Peace was settled on November 27, and the last contingents of both armies finally withdrew. As part of the conditions of separation, the castle of Asahiyama was demolished and the second battle of Kawanakajima came to an end.

Castle Warfare

In order to understand the appearance of a Japanese castle at the time of the samurai, it is necessary to banish from one's mind any image of the beautiful tower keeps of surviving Japanese castles such as Himeji or Matsumoto. Ornate tower keeps did not make their appearance until the 1570s, and the typical *yamashiro* of 1550 would have been a much simpler entity constructed around a series of interconnecting wooded hills. Straightforward wooden stockades linked towers and gates and followed the natural defenses provided by the height and the contours of the mountains. Using the formidable resources in manpower that a *daimyo* could command, adjacent hills were sculpted into a series of interlocking baileys on flat horizontal surfaces, each overlooked by the one above it. The result was a gigantic and bizarre earthwork produced by removing materials rather than piling them up. On top of this framework were placed fences, towers, stables, storehouses, walkways, bridges, and gates. Very little stone was used in the construction except for strengthening the bases of gatehouses and

towers and to combat soil erosion from the excavated slopes. As time went by, the simple palisades and towers inside the *yamashiro* were replaced by stronger wattle and daub walls, plastered over against fire attack, and roofed with tiles as a protection against rain.

From one *honjo* (headquarters castle), a network of satellite castles radiated out, each of which had its own smaller sub-satellite, and with each sub-satellite having its own local cluster of tiny guard posts. The network would be linked visually by a chain of fire beacons. For a *daimyo*'s *honjo*, such as Uesugi Kenshin's Kasugayama, and for most of the satellite castles, a simple stockade was not enough to withstand enemy attack or to provide barracks space for a garrison, so a technique developed whereby the mountain on which the *yamashiro* stood was literally cut to shape.

It was also realized that if the cutaway slopes of the natural hills were reinforced with tightly packed stones arranged scientifically so that any weight upon them was dissipated outward and downward, then much larger, taller, and heavier buildings could be successfully raised on top of them. The result was the introduction of the earliest form of the castle keeps that are now such an attractive feature of extant Japanese military architecture.

At the beginning of the Sengoku period, there were numerous sieges against the pre-stone model of Sengoku *yamashiro*. Arai was taken by the Hojo in 1516 after a desperate fight to control the drawbridge which connected the two halves of this island fortress. It was during the siege of *Un no uchi* in 1536 that Takeda

Ornate tower keeps did not make their appearance until the 1570s.

Above: Hirado Castle, the seat of the Matsuura family, stands guard over the harbor of Hirado on the island of the same name.

Right: The complex outer walls of Himeji Castle as viewed from the top of the keep.

Shingen, then aged 15, had his first combat experience, taking the garrison by surprise after marching through thick snow. The following year, the Hojo besieged the Uesugi Castle of Musashi-Matsuyama, when the garrison tried to summon help from outside by sending a message through the siege lines attached to the collar of a dog. Psychological pressures on a garrison may be noted at the siege of Shika in 1547, where Takeda Shingen had the freshly severed heads of the victims of the battle of Odaihara displayed in front of the castle walls. In each of these cases we may envisage a castle layout with carved hillsides, ditches, and palisades.

Two years later, far away in the south of Japan, Kajiki Castle was captured by samurai of the Shimazu using the newly acquired Portuguese arquebuses, a weapon that was to revolutionize Japanese warfare. When Oda Nobunaga attacked Muraki Castle in 1554 he used a system of rotating volleys of arquebus fire from just across the moat, a pattern that was to become very common in Japanese siege warfare, and was used to tremendous effect from field fortifications at the famous battle of Nagashino in 1575. But even the new arquebuses were not infallible, and the castle of Moji, which occupied a prominent vantage point overlooking the straits of Shimonoseki, changed hands five times between 1557 and 1561 in spite of gunfire, amphibious assault, and even the

Above: The Sakura Gate of Edo Castle, seat of the shogun.

Above: Fukuyama Castle on the coast of the Inland Sea.

Right: The barracks of the *ashigaru* (foot soldiers) in the outer defenses of Kochi Castle. These are probably the only surviving examples in Japan.

bombardment from Portuguese ships described earlier. This was a unique event in Japanese history, and so dramatic was the illustration of the devastating effects of cannonballs against a predominantly wooden fortress that it is surprising that there was so little future development in this direction. The castle of Musashi-Matsuyama enters the story again in 1563 when Takeda Shingen used miners to collapse its walls.

The siege of Minowa in 1566 is one outstanding example of this policy. Minowa Castle in Kozuke was defended fiercely by a strong retainer of the Uesugi called Nagano Narimasa. For this reason Takeda Shingen had left it well alone, but when Narimasa died, fearful lest the Takeda should take advantage of this, the Nagano followers kept his death secret for as long as possible while his heir Narimori consolidated his position.

The Takeda soon realized what had happened and launched their attack in 1566. The great swordsman Kamiizumi Hidetsuna took part in the defense of Minowa with the young heir leading at the front. Attack after attack was repulsed, with the action almost totally

Below: The black castle of Okayama.

Right: The mouth of the well inside
the keep of Matsue Castle.

Left: Nijo Castle in Kyoto was the outposted headquarters of the shogunate in the imperial capital of Kyoto. This is the massive main gate.

Left: Detail from the eaves of the palace of Nijo Castle in Kyoto, one of the most outstanding memorials of the Tokugawa shogunate in the imperial capital of Kyoto.

Right: The walls of
Bitchu-Matsuyama Castle make
good use of the exposed bedrock
beneath them.

concerned with hand-to-hand combat, helped
by some ingenious defense works that included
piles of logs released beside the gate when an
attack took place. Finally, Hidetsuna took the
fight to the Takeda and sallied out of the castle
in a bold surge. The Takeda became
demoralized, but then fate took a hand, for
in another charge by the defenders the young
heir Narimori was cut down and killed. This
time there was no opportunity to keep a commander's death a secret. The Takeda seized
upon this huge psychological weapon, and
the shattered defenders were forced to sue
for peace.

Operations Against Castles of Stone

Stone bases begin to play a part in castle warfare from about 1570 onward. For the up-and-
coming Oda Nobunaga, the decade was
dominated by Japan's longest siege when
he spent ten years, off and on, reducing the
Ikko-ikki's formidable fortress cathedral called
Ishiyama Honganji. This was a long and bitter
campaign directed against a massive *hirajiro*
complex of the latest style situated within a
maze of reed beds and creeks. Supplies were
run to them by sea courtesy of the Mori family,
and the Ikko-ikki also had large numbers of
arquebuses. Their satellite fortress of
Nagashima also held out for years, and on one
occasion an attacking army was caught by
flooding from a broken dyke—a neat reversal of
the conventional siege situation!

Midway through the Ishiyama Honganji

Opposite page: This memorial in
the form of a sleeping samurai is
on top of the mountain that was
the site of the battle of Shizugatake
in 1583.

operation there occurred the celebrated siege of
Nagashino Castle, which withstood several
ingenious attempts to capture it, and was eventually relieved by the famous victory at the
battle of Nagashino. This involved the mass use
of arquebuses firing from behind field fortifications, and although the precise situation of
Nagashino was never repeated, its influence
can be seen in the temporary earthworks raised
by both sides during the Komaki campaign of
1584. The result was stalemate, as neither side
wished to repeat the mistake of Nagashino, and
in fact the battle of Nagakute was fought several miles from the Komaki lines as much as a
result of boredom as anything else. The "trench
system" of Komaki was never seen again in
Japanese history—it just did not fit in with the
samurai ethos, and the only use of earthworks

in future was to augment a castle's stone walls.

Yet every new siege made fresh demands upon the ingenuity of both besiegers and besieged, and the early 1580s saw two very different actions against castles. In 1581 at Tottori, a *yamashiro* with formidable stone walls, the weapon of starvation was used on an unprecedented scale. Kikkawa Tsuneie held out for 200 days, and surrendered only to save his men from having to eat each other. At Shizugatake in 1583, however, the situation was totally different. Shizugatake was one of a chain of Sengoku *yamashiro* raised north of Lake Biwa by Toyotomi Hideyoshi to protect his communications with Kyoto. Little stone was used, and the means of attack adopted by Shibata Katsuie shows a very good understanding of the layout of a Sengoku *yamashiro* complex, because instead of making a frontal assault on the most forward of the castles, he made his way along the connecting ridge to the rear, capturing one castle at a time and then using it as a base for the next attack. The strategy would have succeeded had not Hideyoshi mounted a surprise rescue operation by night, catching Shibata's general unprepared.

Several sieges were involved in Hideyoshi's invasion of Kyushu in 1586, the weapons used ranging from infantry assault to bribery and trickery. The Hojo's mighty Odawara saw the most theatrical siege in Japanese history in 1590, where the besiegers loudly proclaimed their wealth of wine, women, and song to the miserable Hojo defenders cooped up inside. With the Korean invasion of 1592, the Japanese came up against foreign castle styles and siege

Above: The siege of Chinju in Korea, showing the defenders' use of Chinese siege weapons.

techniques for the first time in their history. At first everything went their way. Thousands of arquebuses swept the walls of the Korean fortresses and an assault followed, a pattern that cleared a path as far as Seoul within 20 days. But when the Koreans rallied and the Chinese crossed the border to assist them, the Japanese army was thrown on to the defensive, and had to withstand attacks from within the chain of communications forts they had hastily erected. At Chinju in 1593, however, the Japanese showed that they were able to conduct siege warfare with the same skill as the Chinese when they undermined the fortified town's walls.

By the time of the second invasion in 1597, the only really secure Japanese possessions in Korea were the ring of coastal fortresses called *wajo*, which became the focus for sustained Chinese attacks. Ulsan was only half finished

when it was subjected to human wave assaults in a celebrated winter siege where soldiers from both sides froze to death at their posts. Sunch'on was attacked by sea and land at the same time, with the latter operation making use of the weird and wonderful Chinese siege engines.

There is an amusing anecdote concerning the building of Sach'on Castle in Jozan Kidan, which tells of an argument between the veteran Chosokabe Motochika and a younger samurai about where to place the gun ports in the castle's gatehouse. Chosokabe maintained that gun ports should be inserted "at a level between a man's chest and hips." His colleague disagreed, saying that gun ports should be placed high up on the walls, because low gun ports would allow enemy scouts to peer into the castle. "Let them!" was Chosokabe's reaction, "then they can see how strong it is!"

The lessons from Korea were applied back home in the designs of several fortresses we see today, but on returning to Japan the samurai split into two camps for the succession dispute that culminated in the victory of Sekigahara in 1600. Several key sieges, including Ueda, Otsu, and Fushimi, provided "sideshows" for this decisive battle. Finally, at Osaka in 1614–1615, European techniques of long distance artillery bombardment made their first appearance.

There was a famous siege of the castle of Katsurayama in 1557. Uesugi Kenshin had built Katsurayama Castle in 1553 across the Susohanagawa from Asahiyama to guard the entrance to the passes, so in 1557 Katsurayama itself became Shingen's primary target. Its capture would throw the nearby mountainous areas of Iizuna and Togakushi into Shingen's lap and allow a high-level route into Echigo.

In March 1557, taking advantage of late snow that kept Uesugi Kenshin temporarily confined behind the passes from Echigo, Takeda Shingen's general Baba Nobuharu attacked Katsurayama with 6,000 men in a furious battle that was as much a race against time as anything else. The mountains around were

Above: The sheer size of Kumamoto Castle is shown here by this view of the overlapping stone-clad mounds that make up the castle's encircling walls. The massive keep seems almost dwarfed in the distance.

Above: The keep of Bitchu-Matsuyama Castle, which stands on the highest castle hill in Japan.

themselves covered in snow (the Iizuna area was one of the main skiing centers during the 1998 Winter Olympics), and provided a suitably quiet backdrop to an operation that was savage even by the standards set so far in the Kawanakajima campaign. The garrison of Katsurayama, who were under the command of Ochiai Bitchu no kami, defended the castle desperately, hoping to hold out until the thaw came, and the majority of the defenders eventually died in action. In the numerous *kanjo* (letters of commendation) that Shingen sent out

after the battle he refers to the large number of heads taken at Katsurayama. For example, a samurai from Suwa called Chino Yugeinojo had fought for Shingen at each of his Kawanakajima battles and achieved a total to date of eight enemy heads, of which four were taken at the siege of Katsurayama.

A popular anecdote concerning the fall of Katsurayama tells how the castle's greatest weakness was its lack of a water supply. There was no spring on top of the mountain, so all drinking water had to be carried up from a source near the Joshoji temple on the mountain's lower slopes. This fact was initially unknown to the Takeda troops, and as water was always a crucial factor in a siege the garrison decided to fool the besiegers into thinking that they had ample supplies. As they had plenty of rice the Ochiai soldiers chose a place that was easily visible from the Takeda lines and poured out the white rice in a torrent that looked like a waterfall. It boldly proclaimed the message that this desperately defended castle would be able to hold out until Kenshin broke through.

Unfortunately for the Ochiai, the chief priest of Joshoji betrayed their clever scheme. He passed on to the Takeda the secret information that their only source of water supply in fact lay down beside the temple. Baba Nobuharu's men rushed to occupy the spring and then attacked the castle with renewed confidence. This time they managed to set fire to the castle buildings and the brave castle commander was killed in the attack that followed. There followed a mass suicide by the wives, women, and children of the castle, who flung themselves to their deaths from the crags. The castle burned to ashes, so that "even now when the site is dug, baked rice may be found."

This vivid legend cannot however be linked unequivocally to Katsurayama. There are similar stories told about other sieges, one of which, concerning the siege of Toksan in Korea in 1593, has the defending general washing his horse with white rice. As for finding baked rice on the Katsurayama site, this would be by no means an unusual discovery where a *yamashiro* had

been burned to ashes and taken its rice store with it. Nevertheless, it is clear that Katsurayama fell only after a long and desperate struggle.

Earthworks and Field Fortifications

Field fortifications played a decisive part in the battle of Nagashino in 1575 and the battles of Komaki and Nagakute in 1584. The rival territories of Toyotomi Hideyoshi and Tokugawa Ieyasu met in Owari province, formerly the Oda heartlands, and it was the way in which their antagonism was resolved that was to show the most dramatic influence from the Nagashino experience. Owari province (much of which now lies within the boundaries of the city of Nagoya) was largely flat, so Ieyasu took the opportunity to secure one of the few pieces of high ground, which was the site of the former castle of Komaki, 282 feet (86m) above sea level. As time was pressing Ieyasu's men took to the spade, and raised earth ramparts as Komaki's defenses in a few days. Four other forts were also strengthened to provide secure communications to the south and west.

Hideyoshi soon heard of Ieyasu's activities and responded in kind. Neither of his two front line forts of Iwasakiyama and Nijubori had Komaki's advantage of high ground, so, with memories of Nagashino behind him, he ordered the construction of a long rampart to join the two together. The resulting earthwork, probably strengthened with wood, was completed overnight. It was 2½ miles (2km) long, 13½ feet

A popular anecdote concerning the fall of Katsurayama tells how the castle's greatest weakness was its lack of a water supply.

Above: Toyotomi Hideyoshi, identified by his thousand gourd standard, advances to engage the enemy beside Lake Biwa and is warmly received by friendly locals.

(4.1 m) high, and 7 feet (2.2m) thick, and pierced with several gates to allow a counter attack. The slope of the rampart no doubt also allowed for the provision of firing positions. Satisfied with his Nagashino-like front line, Hideyoshi set up his headquarters to the rear at Gakuden. The following morning, upon observing Hideyoshi's rampart, Ieyasu immediately ordered a similar line to be constructed parallel to it and out from Komaki to the south-east. This was a more modest construction only 2,625 feet (800m) long and anchored on the small fort of Hachimanzuka, from where it was a short distance to his communications forts of Hira and Kobata, but the result was that these two veterans of Nagashino were now facing each other from behind the sixteenth-century equivalent of a World War I trench system.

It was almost inevitable that the lessons of Nagashino should not only have caused these highly skilled generals to take the defensive

measures that they did, but should also prevent either of them from making the first move in attacking each other. The result was stalemate, which was not a situation at all conducive to the samurai spirit, and within a few days there occurred the bloody but indecisive battle of Nagakute. However, Nagakute was not fought between the Komaki lines, but arose from an attempt by one of Hideyoshi's generals to raid Ieyasu's home province while he was sitting in the ramparts of Komaki. As Nagakute was fought some distance away, both armies went back to their lines and stalemate returned. Boredom set in and was relieved by Hideyoshi withdrawing more men to besiege Ieyasu's ally Oda Nobuo in his castle of Kagenoi. In fact no frontal attack between the two ever took place at Komaki. Eventually their differences were settled by negotiation and the ramparts were allowed to crumble back into the rice fields.

The next example of the use of earthworks combined with guns is to be found during Hideyoshi's invasion of Korea in 1592. The rapid advance of the Japanese up the Korean peninsula stalled following the capture of P'yong-yang, which had been defended by stone walls built in the usual Korean pattern of a long, vertical but narrow construction that was not based round an earth core as in the Japanese style. When P'yong-yang came under threat from the expeditionary army sent by the Ming Chinese the Japanese defenders made no attempt to increase the size of the Korean walls. Instead they turned to digging to augment the existing defenses of the city by horizontal earthwork bastions. P'yong-yang therefore

Left: An aerial view of the battle-field of Nagashino. The castle lies at the confluence of the two rivers.

Right: Sakai Tadatsugu, who accompanied Tokugawa Ieyasu in many of his campaigns.

provides the first example of the construction of recognizable Japanese-style fortifications in Korea. The advancing Chinese, who compared the Japanese efforts unfavorably to their own magnificent Great Wall of China, scorned the crude ramparts, referring to them as "earth-caverns," and likened them to the primitive earthworks found among the Jurchids of Manchuria. What the Chinese did not realize was that these "earth caverns" were designed to provide a clear field of fire for thousands of arquebuses, and to absorb whatever punishment the Chinese cannon could throw at them.

In 1614 Japan was again to see an earthwork play a vital role in a battle. When Toyotomi Hideyori repaired and enlarged his late father's castle at Osaka an important addition to the forward defenses was provided in the form of a barbican earthwork called the Sanada-maru after its commander Sanada Yukimura. In front of the Sanada-maru was a wide ditch with palisades on either side and one along the middle of the base. There were wooden towers and walls with a two-story firing platform, and the whole complex bristled with guns. Even though little if any stone was used in its construction, the Sanada-maru held out against one of the first and fiercest attacks of the siege of Osaka.

Head Collection

One of the most persistent samurai traditions was the collection of the severed heads of the enemy. Nothing was more certain to win recognition than the evidence of the enemy's head, proving the samurai's competence in combat.

Captives also usually had their heads cut off, though a victorious commander might pardon the captured vassals on the condition that they become his vassals. Sometimes a captive's entering the priesthood was a condition for sparing his life. Taking ransom in the form of monetary compensation to save the lives of captives, a common practice in Western warfare, was rare in Japanese culture. Likewise, captives becoming slaves, also a common practice in many other societies, was out of the question for the proud professional samurai.

A major victory would always end with the piling up of dozens, even hundreds, of chopped-off heads in the commander's quarters. *Azuma kagami* recorded that the insurrection of Wada Yoshimori in 1213 yielded 234 heads of defeated warriors, which were duly displayed along the banks of the Katasegawa River.

Heiji monogatari describes an episode in which the head of a mortally wounded samurai was cut off by his ally in order to avoid dishonor. When Takiguchi Toshitsune was shot in the neck in battle and had almost fallen from his horse's back, his master said to a vassal, "Don't let Takiguchi's head be taken by the enemy. Bring it to us." Hearing his master's command, Takiguchi voluntarily extended his neck to his fellow samurai, saying, "That eases my mind."

According to custom, the heads of respectable samurai were cleaned and the hair combed before being examined. The cleaning of the decapitated heads sometimes fell to samurai women. A rare eyewitness account, recorded by the daughter of a samurai living in the castle

Nothing was more certain to win recognition than the evidence of the enemy's head, proving the samurai's competence in combat.

Right: The severed head of a samurai's victim is coldly but vividly displayed for all to see in this print by Yoshitoshi.

Opposite page: The head mound at the battle site of Sekigahara.

during a battle yields a description of this repug-
nant operation. The young girl, later known as
Oan, the daughter of the respectable samurai
Yamada Kyoreki, experienced the horror of sleeping beside a collection of severed heads in the
Ogaki Castle of Mino during the great battle of
Sekigahara in 1600. The castle was under constant attack from the superior forces of Tokugawa
Ieyasu. One day, Oan's brother was killed before
her eyes. She was too numb to cry during her
residence in the besieged castle:

> I did not even have a sense of being
> alive—all I could feel was fear and terror.
> But then, afterward, it didn't seem like
> much of anything at all. My mother and I,
> as well as the wives and daughters of the
> other retainers, were in the castle's keep
> casting bullets. Severed heads taken by our
> allies were also gathered up in this area of
> the castle. We attached a tag to each head
> in order to identify them properly. Then
> we repeatedly blackened their teeth. Why
> did we do that? A long time ago, black-
> ened teeth were admired as the sign of a
> distinguished man. So, we were asked to
> apply a generous coat of *ohaguro* [a black
> dental dye] to any heads with white teeth.
> [Tooth-dyeing, a popular practice among
> the ladies of the court in the Heian period,
> was also affected by male aristocrats and
> warriors from the late Heian to the
> Muromachi periods.] Even these severed
> heads no longer held any terror for me. I
> used to sleep enveloped by the bloody
> odor of those old heads.

Right: A samurai leaves the battlefield bearing the severed heads of his enemies.

Oan later narrowly escaped with her family from the doomed fortress. Here it is important to note that, even in the face of imminent defeat, the cosmetic beautification of the heads was regularly carried out.

This act of cleaning the heads was in part a sign of respect for fallen warriors. More to the point, it represented a tribute to the victors' pride as men who could defeat heroic enemies. And the tangible proof of one's prowess, in the form of a pile of severed heads, would certainly result in better rewards from one's lord.

That was the essence of the paradox of the samurai. They were pledged to serve their lords with undying loyalty even unto death. But even the most loyal samurai had to be rewarded, and the presentation of heads became the most dramatic expression of this vital element in samurai culture.

Conclusion

When the gunsmoke cleared after the battle of Tennoji in 1615 and the great siege of Osaka ended in favor of the house of Tokugawa, many samurai lay dead. Among the slaughtered victims on the losing side was a samurai whose surname was Marubashi. His son survived him, and grew up to develop a speciality in teaching others the use of the *naginata*. His name was Marubashi Chuya. He was a man of enormous strength, and he bore a particular grudge against the Tokugawa family for his father's death. Several years after Osaka, Chuya made the acquaintance of another potential rebel against the Tokugawa called Yui Shosetsu. Their plan was ambitious. They plotted to blow up the main gunpowder store in Edo Castle and overthrow the government.

The results of this Japanese version of the Gunpowder Plot were as much a disaster for the perpetrators as for the conspirators in the better known English version. Chuya fell ill with a fever, and in his delirium he blurted out the details of the plot. The Tokugawa government acted swiftly and eliminated both plotters together with their entire families.

The quick collapse of this *ronin* rebellion of 1651 illustrated how much the world of the samurai had changed with the establishment of the Tokugawa peace. Until the coming of the Europeans in the nineteenth century, the samurai would have to live not as active warriors but as salaried officials of a centralized police state. But the perceptive ones among them would surely have realized that change

was the one concept that had characterized the world of the samurai from its very beginning. The challenge from China, the great civil wars of Taira and Minamoto, the Mongol invasions, and the introduction of firearms had all required a response from Japan's warriors. It was only when they could finally not resist the huge pressure from the West that the samurai class disappeared. Until then they had coped as soldiers and administrators. Beyond that point, however, they had no role, and the samurai class passed away into memory, to become no more than a symbol of Japan's glorious military past.

Above: One of the Loyal Retainers of Ako, better known as the 47 *Ronin*, whose carefully planned act of revenge in 1702 entered into Japanese folklore.

APPENDIX

time chart

Prehistoric Japan

10,000 B.C.–A.D. 538

    Jomon period

300 B.C.–A.D. 300

    Yayoi period

A.D. 300–A.D. 700

    Kofun period—large earthen tombs (*kofun*) built

369	Japanese colony of Minana established in Korea
538	Buddhism introduced to Japan
607	Prince Shotoku builds the Horyuji
645	Defeat of the Soga clan
646	Taika Reform

710	First permanent capital at Nara
752	Great Buddha of Nara completed
794	Capital moved to Kyoto
950	Revolt of Taira Masakado
1053	Byodo-In built at Uji
1160	Hogen Rebellion
1180	Battle of Ishibashiyama
	First battle of Uji
	Burning of Nara
	Battle of the Fujigawa

1183	Siege of Hiuchi
	Battle of Tonamiyama (Kurikara)
1184	Second battle of Uji 
	Battle of Awazu
	Battle of Ichinotani
	Battle of Yashima
1185	Battle of Dan no Ura
1189	Battle of Koromogawa
1192	Death of Minamoto Yoritomo
1219	Shokyu Rebellion
	Third battle of Uji
1274	First Mongol invasion of Japan
1281	Second Mongol invasion of Japan 
1331	Revolt of Go-Daigo
	Siege of Kasagi
	Siege of Akasaka
	Siege of Chihaya
1333	Suicide of the Kamakura Hojo
1336	Battle of Minatogawa
1348	Battle of Shijo Nawate 
1392	Accession of shogun Ashikaga Yoshimitsu
1467	Onin War begins
1477	Onin War officially ends
	Fighting spreads to provinces
1480	Hojo Soun supports Imagawa
1493	Hojo capture Izu
1494	Hojo capture Odawara
1506	Ikko-ikki active in Kaga
1512	Hojo capture Kamakura
1518	Siege of Arai
1524	Hojo capture Edo
1536	Takeda Shingen's first battle at Un no kuchi
1537	First battle of Konodai

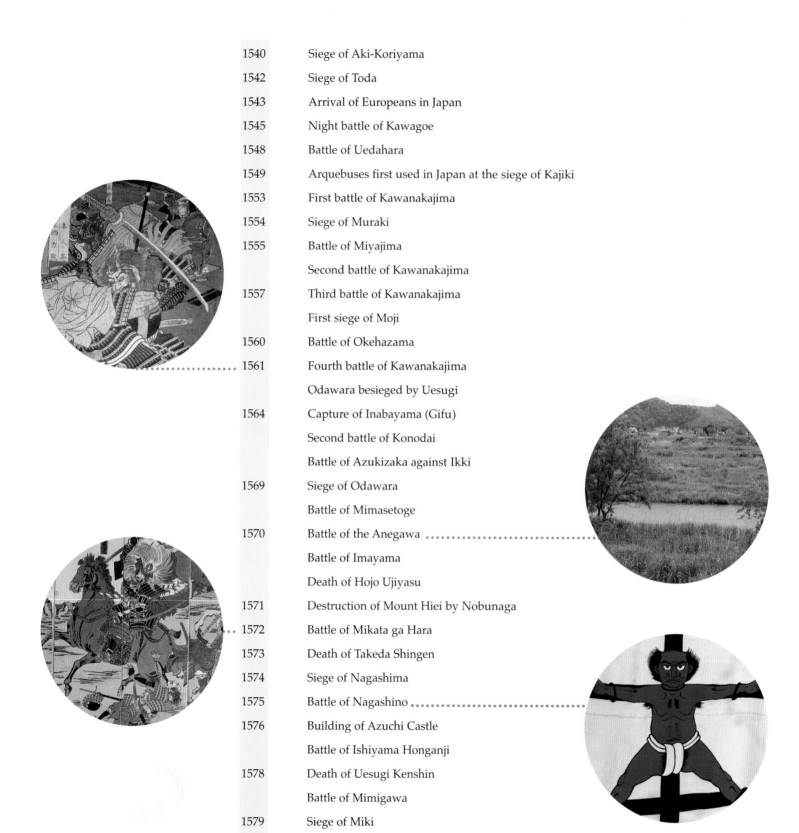

1580	Surrender of Ishiyama Honganji
1581	Siege of Tottori
1582	Death of Takeda Katsuyori
	Murder of Oda Nobunaga
	Battle of Yamazaki 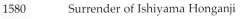 
1583	Battle of Shizugatake
1584	Battles of Komaki and Nagakute
1585	Invasion of Shikoku
1586	Building of Osaka Castle
	Battle of Hetsugigawa
1587	Invasion of Kyushu; Sword Hunt
1590	Siege of Odawara
1591	Siege of Kunoe
	Unification of Japan completed
	Separation Edict
1592	First invasion of Korea
1593	Japanese withdraw from Korea
1597	Second invasion of Korea 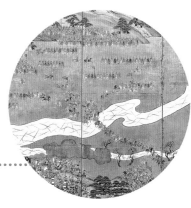
1598	Death of Toyotomi Hideyoshi
	Korean War ends
1600	Battle of Sekigahara
1603	Tokugawa Ieyasu becomes Shogun
1614	Winter Campaign of Osaka
1615	Summer Campaign of Osaka
1616	Death of Tokugawa Ieyasu
1638	Shimabara Rebellion is defeated
1639	Closed-country Edict
1854	Arrival of U.S. ships
1868	Meiji Restoration

BIBLIOGRAPHY

Asakawa, K: *The Documents of Iriki: Illustrative of the Development of the Feudal Institutions of Japan,* Greenwood, Connecticut, 1929 (reprinted 1974).

Aston, W.G. Nihongi: *Chronicles of Japan from the Earliest Times to AD 697,* Tuttle and Co., Vermont, 1972.

Ballard, G.A.: *The Influence of the Sea on the Political History of Japan,* John Murray, London, 1921.

Barker, A.J.: *Suicide Weapon,* Pan Ballantine, London, 1971.

Beasley, W.G.: *The Meiji Restoration,* Stanford University Press, 1973.

Berry, Mary E.: *Hideyoshi,* Harvard University Press, 1982.

Bonar, H.A.C.: *Transactions of the Asiatic Society of Japan,* 1887.

Boscaro, A.: *101 Letters of Hideyoshi,* Sophia University, Tokyo, 1975.

Boxer, C.R.: *Transactions of the Asiatic Society of Japan* (2nd Series), 1931.

Boxer, C.R.: *The Christian Century in Japan: 1549–1650,* University of California Press, Berkeley, 1951.

Cortazzi, Hugh: *Dr. Willis in Japan: British Medical Pioneer 1862–1877,* Athlone Press, London, 1985.

Covell, J.C. and Covell, A.: *Korean Impact on Japanese Culture: Japan's Hidden History,* Hollym, New Jersey, 1984.

Craig, Albert M.: *Choshu in the Meiji Restoration,* Harvard University Press, 1961.

Hall, J.W. (ed.): *The Cambridge History of Japan: Volume 4, Early Modern Japan,* Cambridge University Press, Cambridge, 1991.

Hazard, Benjamin H.: *Monumenta Nipponica,* 1967.

Hazard, Benjamin H.: *Japanese Marauding in Medieval Korea: The Wako Impact on Late Korea,* Unpublished PhD Thesis, University of California, Berkeley, 1967.

Ikegami, Eiko: *The Taming of the Samurai: Honorific Individualism and the Making of Modern Japan,* Harvard University Press, 1994.

Kitagawa, Hiroshi and Tsuchida, Bruce: *The Tale of Heike (Heike Monogatari),* University of Tokyo Press, 1975.

Kuno, Y.S.: *Japanese Expansion on the Asiatic Continent,* University of California Press, Berkeley, 1937.

Mahito, Ishimitsu (ed.): *Remembering Aizu: The Testament of Shiba Goro* (translated with notes by Teruko Craig), University of Hawaii Press, Honolulu, 1999.

Masuda, Wataru: *Japan and China: Mutual Representations in the Modern Era* (translated by Joshua A. Fogel), Curzon Press, 2000.

McCullough, Helen: *The Taiheiki: A Chronicle of Medieval Japan,* Columbia University Press, New York, 1959.

Morris, Ivan: *The Nobility of Failure: Tragic Heroes in the History of Japan,* Secker and Warburg, London, 1975.

Philippi, Donald L.: *Kojiki,* University of Tokyo Press, 1969.

Sadler, A.L.: *The Maker of Modern Japan: The Life of Tokugawa Ieyasu,* Allen and Unwin, London, 1937.

Sadler, A.L.: *Transactions of the Asiatic Society of Japan (2nd Series),* 1937.

Seward, Jack: *Hara-kiri: Japanese Ritual Suicide,* Tuttle, Vermont, 1968.

Smith R.D.: *The International Journal of Nautical Archaeology and Underwater Exploration,* 1988.

Takahashi, K.: *Hata Sashimono,* Akida Shoten, Tokyo, 1965.

Takegoshi, Yosaburo: *The Economic Aspects of the History of the Civilisation of Japan,* London, 1930.

Takegoshi, Y.: *The Story of the Wako,* Tokyo, 1940.

Takenouchi, Kazusai: *Ehon Taikoki,* Kobayashi Rokubei, Osaka, 1802.

Tanaka Taneo: *Japan in the Muromachi Age,* University of California Press, 1977.

Tsunoda, R., de Bary, W., and Keene, D. (eds.): *Sources of Japanese Tradition Volume I,* Columbia University Press, 1958.

Varley, Paul: *Warriors of Japan,* University of Hawaii Press, 1994.

Wilson, William R.: *Hogen Monogatari,* Sophia University Press, Tokyo, 1971.

Yamaguchi, Kohei: *Byakkotai,* Aizu-Wakamatsu City, 1948.

Yamamoto, Tsunetomo: *Hagakure: The Book of the Samurai,* 1979.